AVOWED INTENT

AVOWED INTENT

An Autobiography of Lord Longford

Little, Brown and Company

A *Little, Brown* Book

First published in Great Britain in 1994
by Little, Brown and Company

Copyright © 1994 The Earl of Longford

Extract on page 26 from 'In Memory of Basil, Marquess of
Dufferin and Ava' from *Collected Poems* by John Betjeman
reproduced by kind permission of John Murray
(Publishers) Ltd.

A CIP catalogue record for this book is
available from the British Library.

ISBN 0 316 91089 9

Typeset by M Rules
Printed and bound in Great Britain by
Clays Ltd, St Ives plc

Little, Brown and Company (UK)
Brettenham House
Lancaster Place
London WC2E 7EN

For Elizabeth

ACKNOWLEDGEMENTS

I must express my thanks to begin with to the incomparable Gwen Keeble whose ninetieth birthday we celebrated in the House of Lords on 18 May this year. After that, to Barbara Winch, Jenny Mackilligin, Kitty Chapman, Matthew Oliver whom nothing escapes, and the elegant Maggie Tresadern and the staff of the Susan Hamilton Secretariat, as warm-hearted as they are efficient, all of whom have proved invaluable in the production of this book.

My thanks also to many friends mentioned or not mentioned here: the first names that come into my mind are Lord Shackleton, Leader of the House of Lords; Malcolm Shepherd, Chief Whip and one-time Leader of the House of Lords; Cledwyn Cledwyn, Leader of the Labour Peers for ten years; Ted Graham, Labour Chief Whip; and Geoffrey Ampthill, Lord Chairman of Committees, and his predecessors. The kindness and humour of the devoted staff of the House of Lords at all levels are unforgettable.

Mr and Mrs Lilley preside over us most acceptably in Chesil Court. Gwen Brown and Ellen Grinter supply our every need at Bernhurst, disseminating joy. Elizabeth Maxwell restores me Sunday after Sunday after my jogging walk.

I would also like to thank Mary Craig and Peter Stanford who have written about me in terms that do me far more honour than I deserve.

First and last comes Elizabeth, of whom much is said in this book, but not remotely enough.

CONTENTS

Contents

INTRODUCTION

When I was a tutor at Oxford, I heard of a don at college, who was said by his pupils to have obtained seven second-class honours degrees. True or false, the story provides me with a personal analogy.

Looking back over my eighty-eight years of life, I claim to have achieved second-class (possibly 2/1) honours in six areas, and a borderline first in one.

I was a don at Christ Church, Oxford, but never a professor or head of a college.

I was a cabinet minister, a Leader of the House of Lords, but I never held one of the four or five top offices. I was chairman of a clearing bank, but it was one of the smaller ones.

I was chairman of a publishing house, though not a large or famous one.

I have written more than a score of books, nine of which dealt with religious subjects. My book on Pope John Paul II won the *Universe* prize for the religious book of the year. But in literary circles I have never been placed in the top bracket.

I have been a social worker in the widest sense. I have visited many prisons and countless prisoners. I opened the first debate on prisons in the House of Lords. With the help of others I founded the New Bridge for ex-prisoners and the New Horizon youth centre for homeless young people. I was chairman for a time of the National Society for the Mentally

Handicapped, now called Mencap. However, my achievements are small compared to those of Leonard Cheshire or Sue Ryder, Elie Jansen (who founded the Richmond Fellowship) or Peter Thompson (Matthew Trust).

When a volume of mine appeared in 1953, Raymond Mortimer, chief literary critic of the *Sunday Times,* said of me in a review that was by no means uncritical: 'He is the ideal schoolmaster. He will always find something to like and encourage in the most unattractive and unpopular of boys.'

In the same newspaper, another gifted writer, Alan Brien, called me 'the outcast's outcast'. But for an hereditary earl, a former Leader of the House of Lords and a Knight of the Garter to call himself an outcast would be patent humbug.

I prefer to remember what happened when I was introduced as a new Lord-in-Waiting in 1945 to King George VI.

'Why did you join them?' he asked, obviously meaning the Labour Party.

I discarded as impertinent any idea of saying, 'Because I believe that all human beings are equal in the sight of God.' I replied rather timidly, 'Because I'm on the side of the underdogs.'

'So am I,' said the King, and as the founder and inspiration of the Duke of York's Camp for working-class boys, he was at least as entitled as I was to the claim. However feebly I have stood up for the underdog I have stood where it has been an honour to stand.

My claim to be a borderline first is in the home faculty. I have been happily married for sixty-two years. I have had eight children, one tragically killed in a motoring accident, have a corresponding number of in-laws, twenty-six grandchildren, all delightful, and five great-grandchildren, all delightful. The credit for all this goes almost entirely to my wife, Elizabeth, but a kindly examiner might award me an alpha-beta mark, after a severe viva.

What have been the main circumstances of my formation? Privilege obviously must be mentioned early. The younger son of an Irish earl, educated at Eton and Oxford at my family's expense, I started a long way up the worldly ladder. When I was young, however, I never expected to be made a lord, which I was when I was thirty-nine, or to succeed my brother as earl when I was fifty-five. A further influence, significant but hard to evaluate, cannot be ignored. Our family house in County Westmeath, now called Tullynally Castle by my son Thomas, to whom it passed at my brother's death, was my boyhood home. I have at no time in my life failed to describe myself as Irish. When a member of the British cabinet in 1965, I visited Lansdowne Road with President de Valera for the rugby international, I shouted for Ireland, to the possible embarrassment of my staff. I wear with pride the Irish Rugby Union tie (Triple Crown 1982), given me by an Ulster Protestant.

In 1935, I published *Peace by Ordeal*, my history of the Irish Treaty of 1921, which has stood the test of time and has recently been republished for the fifth time. Today I cannot but believe that, in spite of my Ascendancy background, my Irishness has offered a deep support to my Roman Catholicism.

In the Attlee government of 1945–51 I held various positions of increasing importance, finishing as First Lord of the Admiralty, just outside the cabinet. But it was when I was Minister for the British Zone of Germany, 1947–8, under the Foreign Secretary, Ernest Bevin, that my Christian professions were tested to the full. By the time I became Minister, I was profoundly imbued with the idea that we must apply Christian principles in our dealings with the defeated and half-starving Germans. At this time, if ever in my life, my guidance seemed to come from above.

In the world below I was much influenced by Bishop Bell of Chichester, Dick Stokes, MP, and above all by the publisher and Socialist Victor Gollancz, who had a unique power to stir and provoke my conscience.

At any rate, when I went out to Germany in May 1947, I proclaimed far and wide the message that we, the British government, stood for Christian principles. I aroused considerable controversy at home when I told a classroom of fainting German schoolchildren: 'You are absolutely right to be proud of being German.' I told all and sundry that we ought to pray for the Germans, which led Ernest Bevin, a great man in his own earthy way, to say humorously: 'With you and

Stafford [Cripps, a great Christian Socialist] in the government, we are neglecting no source of supply.'

But the conflict between the gospel that I was so proudly
proclaiming and the official policy of the four allies, Britain,
USA, France and Russia, was at that time fundamental,
although a year or two later it would have been different. I was
really a kind of impostor, if a well-meaning impostor. I tried to
extricate myself from a false position by letters of resignation,
arguing at length with Clem Attlee, the Prime Minister, whom
later on I came to describe as an ethical giant. His replies
always took the same form: 'My dear Frank, thank you for your
note. I will see you as soon as it becomes possible.'

After a good deal of this kind of thing, I allowed myself,
weakly perhaps, to be kicked upstairs in May 1948, and to
become Minister of Civil Aviation. I never stopped protesting.
As a Christian, however, during this period I can only say that
the spirit was willing, but the flesh was weak.

In 1953, after the fall of the Attlee government, I published
my first volume of autobiography, *Born to Believe*, in which I
reaffirmed unequivocally my Christian beliefs.

In the thirteen 'wasted' years of Tory rule, 1951–64, I
espoused a number of great causes. I had become a prison visitor in Oxford in the late thirties; I opened the first debate on
prisons held in the House of Lords in 1955, initiated the New
Bridge for ex-prisoners in the same year and not long afterwards published a book on *The Causes of Crime*. Of all that I
hope I can feel reasonably proud, but must admit that my
Christianity was adjusted on occasion to the requirements of
my so-called career.

As a cabinet minister I cannot feel that I struck a Christian
note of any importance. My position was in fact very weak – the
only cabinet minister apart from the Lord Chancellor in the
House of Lords. But at least when the Abortion Law Reform
Bill came along I left my seat and spoke against it from the
back benches. When I finally resigned in January 1968 on an
education issue, I cannot pretend that Christianity came into
it directly, although my concern for the young was thoroughly
Christian, if not confined to Christians.

Since resigning from government, I have been associated

with many social initiatives There was a time when I was best known for my anti-pornography activities.

'I know you're Lord Porn,' a taxi driver said to me, 'but what's your other name?' I have never faltered from my opposition to pornography, but my record in that field does not begin to compare with that of the great champion Mary Whitehouse. Cecil King said at the time that it was not my scene, and I have to admit that there was a good deal of truth in that.

I have not been outstandingly good in loving the sinner but I have been much weaker in hating the sin. No one who has lived through a century when six million Jews were murdered by the Nazis and perhaps as many Russians under Stalin can shut his eyes to the terrible atrocities that can be committed by men. I hope that when the reader reaches the sections of this book dealing with penal reform he will realise that a civilised society is, in my view, impossible without just punishments. But the main emphasis of my life has lain elsewhere.

June 1994

1
GROWING UP

When I was just nine years old, in 1915, I was sent away to Furzieclose preparatory school in Hampshire, near New Milton and therefore near the sea. It seems strange to me now that I was sent away so early, but at the time it seemed completely natural. I had been well educated by a governess who taught me and my clever sisters, Pansy and Mary, and by a local clergyman who taught me Latin. I was considered a very clever little boy.

By the time I was ten I was in the top division, and when my older brother Edward went to Eton I was more or less head of the prep school. I was good at mathematics; indeed in those early years I was ahead of Henry Whitehead, later a famous professor of geometry. I admit that he was fast overtaking me when he left the school; he certainly defeated me in the final of the school boxing competition.

In the following year I was again in the final of the boxing, and this time I thought that I had won. After the third round I lay back happily on my stool in front of a large audience of wounded soldiers. Pointing to my adversary, I said to my second, 'It looks all right, he's covered with blood.'

The second, an old hand, knew better. 'Wait till they wipe it off,' he said. And sure enough it was my blood, not his. The referee stepped forward and held aloft the arm of my conqueror, Alan Griffiths. 'Griffiths is the winner,' he proclaimed.

I gave up boxing soon after I went to Eton. I wanted neither to hurt nor be hurt sufficiently to enjoy it. I continued wrestling for quite a few years.

Alan, who died quite recently, went on to achieve spiritual glory. When I next caught sight of him (on television many years later) he had become Father Bede Griffiths with beautiful white hair and a long white beard. He had lived for a long time in an Indian ashram reconciling Christians and Hindus with remarkable success. Two of his books have become classics.

Many people think of public schools as hotbeds of homosexual activity. This certainly was not my experience, although my older brother suffered a most unfortunate encounter. I well remember the painful occasion when my mother had to tell me that Edward had been sexually assaulted in the bath at Eton. She, a widow with six children, had been consulted as to whether the aggressor ought to be allowed to remain at the school. She had bravely agreed to his remaining, but stipulated that my brother should not be expected to fag for him. The boy was later caught in the same kind of illicit activity and removed from the school. Later again, he became a respected figure in county life and a first-class cricketer.

My illustrious friend (Professor) Leslie Rowse told my daughter Antonia on one occasion that he was very fond of me but regretted that I had not had any homosexual experience. He was no doubt contrasting me with a number of the famous intellectuals who were at Oxford in my time. The biographers of Evelyn Waugh and Cyril Connolly have admitted that these writers each had a homosexual period.

It may be that the frightening news about my brother gave me a subconscious fear of homosexualism. I can, however, plead in return that I was the first public man to espouse the findings of the Wolfenden Report in 1956, which I did when I opened a debate in the House of Lords. The report, which became law many years later, recommended that homosexual relations in private between consenting adults should no longer be a criminal offence.

The headmaster of our preparatory school, Philip Stubbs –

known to the boys as 'Tubby' – got a lot out of his pupils with the help of a peculiarly sardonic humour. One morning the school was assembled with the solemnity that betokened the commission of a major crime.

'I should like to know the names,' said Tubby slowly, 'of those young men who have been what they call "bagging a few of Tubby's goosegogs" – what others would call stealing the headmaster's gooseberries.'

Complete and prolonged silence. Not a soul moved. If Tubby hoped to spot the criminals by their look of shame his histrionics seemed to have defeated his purpose, for every boy in the school was blushing to the roots of his hair.

'I think I ought to tell you,' went on Tubby deliberately, 'that those gooseberries were poisoned – poisoned against rats. I repeat rats. The poison is guaranteed to produce an extremely unpleasant death – I should imagine that it would begin to operate just about now.'

By this time on half a dozen countenances it was beginning to be possible to detect extremes of guilt and terror. Tubby seemed about to leave the room then, as if remembering something, turned back.

'I almost forgot to mention that there is just one way of saving your beastly skins. If none of you is interested in that, your parents may be – though I cannot imagine why. A small supply of the only existing antidote is in the hands of the matron—'

Before he had finished, six panic-stricken boys had fled from the room. Tubby was in the matron's room almost as soon as they were, and the only antidote they received was a regulation dose with his 'bicycle belt'.

Only once did I receive this kind of chastisement. I was accused, no doubt correctly, of promoting a fight between the only American boy and the only Italian boy in the school. I can still see from between my legs Tubby's face as the bicycle belt descended. At the time I thought that he was enjoying it. But he was a kindly man and it may well have hurt him more than it hurt me.

It would be difficult to say whether I was unhappy or happy at preparatory school. All of us used to cry regularly as we

8

drove back to school at the beginning of each term in the station 'fly'. We went through this ceremony even when returning to school for the last time, but it never occurred to me, or any of us, I imagine, to think that there was a better way of life.

There was a good deal of minor bullying. Most of us suffered at one point or another. I remember suddenly feeling alone in a classroom. A smirking youngster entered and told me, 'You are wanted in the boot hole.' Thither I repaired, to be covered with pinches which were more humiliating than painful. But by and large, I was 'one of the boys', though I like to think I never pinched anyone in the boot hole.

Furzieclose was not in those days an intellectual academy. No one in my time got a scholarship at a public school. We were delighted when a boy got into Osborne, the naval training college. Yet Henry Whitehead and Alan, later Bede, Griffiths, achieved high distinction later. So indeed did the Trevelyan brothers – John becoming film censor and Humphrey (Bunny because of the size of his ears) ambassador in Moscow and elsewhere and Knight of the Garter. Whether or not I could have won a scholarship at Eton remains doubtful. Edward almost certainly could have. Our mother, however, took the somewhat old-fashioned view that we were sufficiently well off not to try to take the bread out of the mouths of the poorer boys.

No one, surely, could claim that I have proved a predictable product of my background. The Pakenham family was very much part of the Irish Protestant Ascendancy, and had a long military tradition. The Duke of Wellington married my great-great aunt Kitty, whom she continued to love although his treatment of her was somewhat chilly. Kitty's brother, General Pakenham, was killed leading the British troops at New Orleans in 1815. My father was killed leading his brigade at Gallipoli in 1915. My elder brother, Edward, however, adopted a different attitude to military affairs. He was the first boy after the war of 1914–18 to insist on leaving Officers' Training Corps, which was then treated as compulsory at Eton. The College Chronicle remarked at the time, not quite accurately:

9

'As you were,' the sergeants shouted,
'As you were,' the sergeants swore.
'They've taken Private Longford
And they've hurled him from the corps.'

My eldest sister Pansy married Henry Lamb, a leading artist much older than herself. In old age, as a widow, she became a Catholic and at the time of writing has found a beautiful vocation in showing visitors round St Peter's in Rome. My second sister married the very good-looking possessor of a splendid house in Herefordshire, who was killed in the war in a fashion worthy of my father. My third sister married the distinguished novelist Anthony Powell. My fourth sister died prematurely of cancer; her husband was a dashing old Etonian, an outstanding amateur race rider. Her son edits the *Times Literary Supplement* today. If there be in the family a common thread, where heredity and environment were so similar and yet the results so different, frankly, it eludes me.

My father was the fifth Earl of Longford, an Irish landlord, his Majesty's Lieutenant for County Longford. Our family home is what my son, the present owner, calls Tullynally Castle. We called it Pakenham Hall. My cousin, Ivor Pakenham, a recognised genealogist, has worked out a family tree which traces us back to a certain 'Walter', founder of the Church of Pakenham, County of Suffolk c.1100. A certain Henry Pakenham, captain of foot, was the first to establish the family in Ireland in the seventeenth century, being rewarded by Cromwell for specified exploits with what is now the Pakenham Estate in Westmeath. Irish Baron of Longford was granted 1756; an Irish Earldom of Longford in 1785. An English Baron of Silchester, confirming a seat in the House of Lords, followed in 1821.

Among the later Pakenhams, politicians are conspicuously absent, although my father's father was an undersecretary at the War Office. As far as I can judge, Catholics are absent also, with one glorious exception. Charles Reginald Pakenham gave up his commission in the Grenadier Guards and became a Catholic monk. The family as a whole do not seem to have been pleased about it, but his uncle, the Duke of Wellington, continued to take a kindly interest in him.

'Well, Charles,' he said, 'you have been a good soldier. Strive to be a good monk': and a good monk he proved. As Paul Mary Pakenham he founded the Passionist Order in Ireland, and though he died at thirty-six he left behind him such a reputation for sanctity that his beatification has been eagerly hoped for.

My father's mother was Selina Rice (now spelt Rhys), an heiress of the House of Dynevor of Llandilo, in Carmarthenshire. Whoever accuses me of lacking Celtic blood on my Irish side is foxed by the authenticity of my Welsh credentials.

My mother, born in 1877, and thirteen years younger than my father, was Mary Child-Villiers, daughter of the seventh Earl of Jersey. My grandfather was at one time Governor of New South Wales, and at another Paymaster-General. Although he died in 1915, I find he is still very well remembered as Lord Lieutenant of Oxfordshire and High Steward of Oxford, in which capacities his public spirit and beneficence were unsurpassed.

No blood, we learn from a well-known essay by Lord Keynes, is to be found distributed more liberally than the Villiers blood among the great houses in Britain.

My mother's mother, daughter of Lord Leigh of Stoneleigh, Warwickshire, was a leading political and literary hostess, a Dame of the British Empire, the President of the Victoria League; by all accounts a public speaker of the highest class, whether in the Conservative interest or on wider topics.

She was friends with such men as Stevenson, Kipling, Gosse, Kitchener, and Conservative statesmen of various kinds. She gladly welcomed Joseph Chamberlain, my wife's great-uncle, in his later phase, though she records how her butler conveyed discreet disapproval when she invited him to dinner. When I visited her during the Second War she was fully aware, though well over ninety, of the situation and issues. But she admitted that it seemed strange to have Russia on our side. 'You see, the first war I remember was the Crimean War and we had her against us then.'

Various first-hand accounts have been given of my father's

11

last hours, when he led his brigade at Suvla Bay against an impregnable Turkish position. Lord Burnham says of him, 'Longford knew where he wanted to get to and walked straight there at the head of his brigade under a very heavy fire with this walking stick in his hand.' Anthony Rothschild reported: 'It was here that the Brigadier was killed just getting out of the last trenches; he had disdained to take cover all day and seemed to bear a charmed life. He certainly gave courage to all who were near him by his example.' Did he pass any of it on to me? I hesitate to make so audacious a claim.

I shall be referring more than once in these pages to the influence of my uncle Arthur Villiers, merchant banker and presiding genius of the Eton Manor Club in East London for half a century. One other relative must on no account be omitted – Lord Dunsany, Uncle Eddie, who married my mother's younger sister Beatrice, whom we saw a great deal as children. A mighty store of tradition and anecdote has grown up around him in my family.

Acquaintance in a club: 'I say, Dunsany, you're an Irishman aren't you? Do you know —— [a new Irish minister]?' Uncle Eddie: 'Oh hullo, you're an Englishman, aren't you? Did you know Crippen?'

Brilliant Oxford don on visit to Pakenham (after prolonged reading aloud of modern poetry): 'What do you think of that, Lord Dunsany? Pretty good stuff, isn't it?' Uncle Eddie: 'For years people in England have been saying that poetry's rot, and now at last it is'.

Uncle Eddie, cleaning his rifle in the drawing room: 'Throw up that window, will you.' Bang, a bullet whistles past and a rabbit falls dead in the park.

I was staying with him at Dunsany at the time of the Tailteann games, the Irish National Championships which included every kind of literary contest under the alleged control of W.B. Yeats. If I remember rightly, Uncle Eddie got no prize at all for plays, short stories or poetry, and a third prize for novels – which he thought more insulting than none. 'Beatrice,' he called across the breakfast table, 'find me a competition where Willie Yeats isn't the judge.' My aunt, after a moment's reflection, said, 'I don't think he is judging the chess.' 'Well, get the blacksmith up here; he used to play a decent game.' And I need hardly say that Uncle Eddie went on the win the Irish Chess Championships.

It is hard to convey the peculiar kind of privilege we enjoyed as children. There was the castle in Westmeath, then called Pakenham Hall, with its beautiful grounds. From 1911 when my father, who had commanded the Second Life Guards, assumed command of the Oxfordshire, Buckinghamshire and Berkshire Yeomanry, there was North Aston Hall, fourteen miles north of Oxford. Before 1914 I suppose there were about fourteen members of staff at Pakenham Hall, a smaller number at North Aston Hall.

After my father's death we lived much more modestly, though a butler was always regarded as a necessity. Although there was a large farm attached to the Castle (now Tullynally), we never were permitted cream.

I was told by my mother that I would have been unlikely to have been in a position to marry except that my great-aunt Caroline, recently widowed, intended to leave me her house, Bernhurst, at Hurst Green, in Sussex, provided that I was called Francis after her late husband.

For good or for ill I learnt early that any success in life must be achieved by my own efforts. In spite of our aristocratic connections we were never in the least degree smart. After my father's death we received hardly any visitors outside the family.

2
ETON

Time ever flowing
Bids us be going
Dear Mother Eton
Far from thee.

Hearts growing older
Love never colder
Never forgotten
Shalt thou be.

'Eton, the Queen of all the schools of all the world'

GLADSTONE

Having become a Roman Catholic and sent four sons to
Ampleforth, a Catholic public school, not to mention having
become a Socialist, I have been inclined to describe myself as
a lapsed old Etonian, but I cannot disguise the thrill I received
quite recently on being invited to be drawn for a gallery of distinguished old Etonians. I have never said and never would say
a word against Eton, so I suppose that my heart is still in the
right place.

When I arrived at Eton I was twelve and a half, the youngest
boy in the school. This fact was to influence, on the whole
harmfully, my whole life at Eton. I always assumed that without
trying very hard I would reach the top. Within my own House
it worked out that way; I was eventually captain of the House
and captain of the House football team for two years. In my
last year as captain we won the House football cup which was,
though hard to believe now, for me a total fulfilment.

I had always assumed, however, that by virtue of automatic
progress upwards I would be captain of the Oppidans – in

other words, top of the thousand boys who were not scholars (known to us as 'tugs'). I can still remember the appalling shock in my last years when I discussed with my greatest friend outside my House the question of whether he would get into Pop (a glamorous society elected by the boys) in the following half. Rather complacently I remarked that in my case it would be automatic as I would be captain of the Oppidans. He paused, and then broke the news to me: 'Bridge [a boy of over nineteen] is staying on.' I, trying to recover, suggested, 'I suppose that I might be elected anyway.' He paused again, then felt bound to tell me, 'I think you ought to know that you are the most unpopular boy in the school'. I had been thinking the same of him, but that did not console me. In the event neither of us was elected to Pop.

In telling that story I am in danger of creating a false impression. I was very happy in my House and in my 'division' – my form. As I went up the school I was usually working with the cleverest boys, particularly the scholars, with whom I got on extremely well, being something of a class humorist. Eton was an extraordinary place in the sense that the number of boys one knew was very small. For example, I never knew of the existence of an exact contemporary, my future brother-in-law Antony Powell, who later became the most distinguished writer of my Eton period.

I left Eton with no kind of chip on my shoulder, but deep down, I suppose, with a determination to make a better mark at Oxford.

Life in our House was dominated by the games ethic and particularly by cricket. Our housemaster, a brilliant scholar, had played cricket for the Gentlemen of England and Middlesex. His great friend, 'Plum' Warner, captain of England and also of Middlesex, lived at Datchet and came over frequently. His son, Esmond, became my lifelong friend.

Many stories are told about my Housemaster, C.M. Wells, called the Bummy Wells by everyone except the members of his House in my time. Like the stories about F.E. Smith, whom I shall talk about later, they make him out to have been rather unpleasant. In fact he was every bit as much a 'fun' man as the first Lord Birkenhead. We enjoyed his deflation of school personalities.

The Keeper of the Field (captain of the school football XI) called one morning on Wells in the Pupil Room to ask permission for one of his House to leave Pupil Room early to play in a match. Wells put him in his place severely. 'Take a seat, my good fellow,' he said to him, and repeated, 'Take a seat, my good fellow,' whenever the captain renewed his plea.

On one occasion, bowling against the school, he decided that the batsman had occupied the crease long enough. 'Throw the ball up to me,' he told him, and when this was done he whipped round on the umpire and said, 'How's that for handling the ball?' The umpire had reluctantly to give the batsman out. However, Wells sent for the boy later that day and gave him a cricket bat as a reminder not to be caught out so easily again.

He was outspokenly unmusical, but was idolised and much imitated by John Christie, who founded Glyndebourne. In an early brochure, Christie began a description of the wines available with the words, 'It all began with Wells,' who was a recognised connoisseur. But when Wells actually attended an opera at Glyndebourne, he left after the first act with his fingers in his ears, demanding, 'Can't someone stop that caterwauling?'

Some years after Wells's death I was invited to stay with John Christie at Glyndebourne, and I gathered that a number of old admirers of Wells were being invited for the weekend to discuss his educational theories. I was a little puzzled by the invitation, as Wells would have been horrified by the idea of educational theories.

Glyndebourne is not so very far from where I live in Sussex. I made my way over on the bus and was greeted by John Christie in person. In some dismay, I blurted out, 'You must be terribly busy with this large number of guests coming for the weekend.'

He replied, 'Not at all; you're the only one who has accepted.' So, rather like one of Evelyn Waugh's heroes in Central Africa, I found myself closeted along with John Christie for the weekend. He was the most genial of hosts but I was relieved when Elizabeth came over on Sunday to rescue me.

Within a day or two of my arrival at Eton, I fielded long leg to the fast bowling of our junior cricket captain G.O. (Gubby) Allen, Allen Geo as Wells always called him, who later captained England. Allen was always extremely kind to me, many years later proposing me for my golf club which, as I was a Labour minister at the time, probably did not enhance his popularity. On our first encounter, he retained his equanimity even when the ball trickled through my legs to the boundary and spoilt his average.

I captained our junior House cricket XI and once, in the semi-final of the championship, went to bed deliriously happy, with 86 not out to my credit. The next day I reached 96, and glory beckoned. An injudicious swipe, however, although I was known as a 'poke', led to a fatal rattle behind me. I never did much good at cricket again. A stupid reluctance to wear glasses handicapped me.

Looking back, it is strange that I did so little work at Eton. I simply basked in the notion that my final triumph was inevitable. For two years, however, I was in the 'division' of the Headmaster, the Reverend C. A. Alington; inspiring as a teacher, still more as a preacher. I can still remember whole passages from his sermons on Sunday evenings. They came back to me when, on behalf of the *Daily Telegraph*, I covered Eton's 550th anniversary celebrations and attended the College chapel. Martin (Lord) Charteris, the Provost, substituting, it seemed to me, for Alington, rose to the occasion magnificently.

Other Eton sermons also linger in my memory. There was a missionary who finished his sermon each year with a ringing appeal, 'It's not your money I want, though God knows I need it. It is you, my dear fellows, you.' We came to know the ending so well that we used to chant it in unison with him. There was a German chaplain, fairly soon after the war, who moved us all with his tribute to the young men who had been at various schools, Eton included, not long before. 'Those splendid young Subalterns of yours, they could not teach us how to fight, for they did not know the way, but they could teach us and they did teach us, the way to die.'

17

But no sermon has stayed with me more powerfully than one of Alington's, which began, 'It was on just such an evening as this, my last at Shrewsbury [where he had been Headmaster], that a boy from the school sat on a bench in the playing fields and a lady of the town came and sat beside him. She began a conversation with the words, "Coming home, dearie?" He straightened himself and replied coldly, "We don't do that sort of thing at Shrewsbury." '

Now came the punchline. 'Not only', said Alington, 'did they do a lot of that kind of thing at Shrewsbury, but he had been expelled for doing it that very day.' He paused, and blew out the candles, with the words, 'Goodnight, and don't forget to pray for your Headmaster.'

If I call myself a Christian today I can never express sufficient gratitude to the influence of Cyril Alington, although I defected from the Church which he served so brilliantly and so long.

A few speculative words should perhaps be added about the effect on me of going to Eton. With my family background it was inevitable that I should go to a public school. But my father went to Winchester, I sent my four sons to Ampleforth, and ten of my grandsons have already passed through public schools without any of them going to Eton. It can still be argued, I believe, that the higher staff ratios assist academic progress at public schools and that corporate loyalty and team spirit are actively inculcated. This is not to deny that these last qualities can be acquired in full measure in the Services, or for that matter, in a mining community. But Eton? Does Eton impose a special mark?

It is generally assumed that it does, but opinions differ widely as to how that mark is to be defined or assessed. Loyal old Etonians will be grateful for the self-confidence they acquired at the school. Plenty of non-Etonians discover in its products an unpleasing arrogance. In my time the religious note was strongly proclaimed with Chapel every morning, twice on Sunday, and the inspiring sermons already referred to.

Does being an old Etonian assist one to achieve worldly

success? The answer was certainly 'yes' until recently. Since the war there have been three old Etonian prime ministers – Eden, Macmillan (a 'Tug') and Home. None of the last five prime ministers, including Margaret Thatcher, went to a public school. When Douglas Hurd, a brilliant scholar who captained the school, stood against John Major for the leadership of the Conservative Party he played down his old Etonian image, arguing that he had been a scholarship boy. Nevertheless he and the equally brilliant William Waldegrave (Fellow of All Souls) continue to represent Eton in the cabinet. Hurd has seen to it that four of the six ministers at the Foreign Office (July, 1993) are old Etonians. The ideal expressed in *Floreat Etona* is not dead yet.

If I were not a Catholic, and if I could afford it, I think that I would follow the example of my sons, who sent their boys to Westminster and Winchester. But if a son of mine went to Eton and eventually modelled himself on Alec Home without necessarily becoming prime minister I would be more than proud.

If I were a self-made tycoon, what Alan Clark would call a 'nouve', I think I would wish to send my son to Eton to obtain for him a social acceptability denied to me. I should warn him, however, that the entrance examination is now a very different affair from what it was in my day when no one of good social origin was ever rejected.

3
OXFORD

'Beautiful Oxford, so venerable, so lovely, so unravaged by the fierce intellectual life of the century, so serene. Thy ineffable charm keeps ever calling us to the true goal of all of us, to the ideal, to perfection.' Matthew Arnold expresses far better than I can much of my feeling about Oxford. But I demur at the reference to her remoteness from the 'fierce intellectual life of the century', at least in my time as a don. That could conceivably have been argued as applying to the Oxford of my undergraduate days in the 1920s, but not to the Oxford of my active period as a don and city councillor, 1932–9. The opposite was somewhat frantically the case.

Another quotation, this time from H. W. Nevinson, sticks in my mind. Nevinson was describing his feelings after his admired friend Roger Casement had been hanged for treason in 1916. Nevinson repaired to Oxford and found her unchanged. ' "I am the mother of holy hope," cried Wisdom in an ancient book. And Oxford for all her preciosity and her absurd self-importance, is always that to me. But she is also', he added, 'the mother of consolation.' His words will come home to many lifelong lovers of Oxford.

I cannot help adding the words used by Gladstone when he was more or less on his deathbed and received a message of goodwill from Oxford. 'There is no message of Christian goodwill,' he replied, 'that I would rather receive than one from the ancient University of Oxford, the God-fearing, God-sustaining University of Oxford. I have served her, mistakenly perhaps, to the best of my ability. My heartfelt prayers are hers, to the uttermost and to the last.'

My love of Oxford has never been confined to the university. As I have explained, when my father took command of the Oxfordshire, Bucks and Berks Yeomanry, my parents acquired North Ashton Hall, not far from Oxford and about seven miles from my mother's old home, Middleton Park, near Bicester. For ten years before I went up to New College, Pakenham Hall remained my ultimate home, but Oxfordshire was very much my English county. In later years I became an Oxford city councillor and parliamentary candidate for the city. My family lived in Oxford from 1934 to 1947.

Readers may understand my thrill when I was asked to join a committee to assist in raising funds for the university. When I was a guest at the encoenia, Elizabeth and I received honourable places. We took it in good heart that our old friend and publisher George Weidenfeld was seated two rows in front of us. I am happy to think that he is vice-chairman of the committee of which I am a humble member.

Nobody who has lived the life of an undergraduate in any college or any country will expect me to sum up the benefits of the atmosphere of free and friendly discussion. I will pick out a few points as they occur to me.

Brilliant friends of mine like Dick Crossman and Douglas (now Lord) Jay appear to give much credit for their intellectual development to W. B. Joseph. His remorseless posing of the question, 'What do you mean by . . .?' anticipated by many years C.E.M. Joad, who made the formula famous on the Brains Trust during the war. I could not help being amused when my Christ Church colleague and long-time friend 'Prof' Lindemann retorted at a philosophical seminar, 'What do you mean by mean?'

Personally, I gained more from A.H. Smith, the second philosophy tutor, who ranked much lower in academic estimation but who later became Warden of New College. Smith, who had been a civil servant, knew all about simplifying complicated issues. 'Rousseau', he used to say, 'asked himself this

21

question: "Why have I got this feeling that I ought to obey the law?" ' Then after a certain amount of beating about the bush he would proceed to give an answer considerably clearer and wiser than any Rousseau provided.

But I gained more still from an unusual Scotsman, H.K. Salvesen, my economics tutor. He was a former army officer and a member of a distinguished whaling family. He returned to Edinburgh after a short spell as a don. The academic life, which thrilled him, fatigued him excessively, as he tortured himself to arrive at the truth. By the end of the term he told me that he could not see across the quad.

Salvers, as we called him, destroyed any last residue in me of Etonian conceit and introduced me to the joy and perils of 'sustained analysis', a phrase that I never heard on the lips of anyone else and will always associate with him.

Whatever my deficiencies on the aesthetic side, then and later, I came to display a considerable power of abstract thought. In a perfect mind, such as has never been possessed by man or woman, the analytic gift would figure, though not perhaps very prominently. In the case of Martin D'Arcy (whom I shall discuss later), J.M. Keynes and Beveridge, this gift carried the horse up to the fence, and left it to genius to bring about the leap. In the Greats and Modern Greats schools at Oxford, analytic ability was certainly an invaluable asset. I had indeed selected to read Modern Greats (philosophy, politics and economics) because it enabled me to atone for the locust years and start level with my cleverest contemporaries.

In the final schools I came a comfortable first without a viva. I got my best marks in Moral and Political Philosophy, the subjects to which I had devoted the least attention. I fancied at that time that I had gone more deeply into economic theory than any of my Oxford contemporaries. In the event Economic Theory was the only subject where I failed to obtain an alpha of any kind.

In my last year I certainly concentrated on achieving a first-class degree, but I developed at the same time a genuine passion for economics which lasted for several years after I left the university. This was before the days of Keynes's General Theory. We spent a lot of time on now forgotten writers like

Cassell. For Banking and Currency, my special subject, we turned to Denis Robertson, like Keynes a luminary of Cambridge.

I should mention perhaps that my first contact with Modern Greats had been hardly encouraging. Lionel, Lord Robbins, (later Professor) was deputising for Salveson. When I first applied to read this school I am afraid I must have appeared a brutal, licentious and flippant old Etonian floating patronisingly from one subject to another. He handed me a list of books, and for want of anything better to say I said, 'They sound rather dull.' (How tactless one can be at the age of nineteen.) 'Don't you like dull books?' said Lord Robbins. 'I should have thought they would rather have appealed to you.'

Later I worked for a time at LSE under Robbins and became an admiring friend many years later in the House of Lords. And, as I say, economics for quite a while became my passion, which was a fact not unimportant not only for my political development.

Soon after I went up to New College I met Evan Durbin, who was to have more influence on me than any other layman outside my family. Durbin later told me that he 'hated the sight of me' in the junior common room at New College. He thought he saw in me all the arrogance and stupidity of the privileged classes. Somehow he got me into an argument which ended with him saying, 'Man, have you ever been hungry?' which shook me slightly. Later I accused him of never having been hungry himself, as the son of a non-conformist minister, who came to Oxford from Taunton, a public school.

From that time on I was never oblivious or ignorant of the Labour case, in humanitarian terms, but my intensive though still very juvenile study of economics tended to confirm me in the position that I already had. In a nutshell, I was able to believe for nearly ten years after I first met Evan Durbin that the doctrine of inequality plus private enterprise was better calculated than that of equality plus planning to raise the general standard of life. I was able to tell him, therefore, with genuine sadness in my voice that I, far more than he, was going to improve the condition of the working class and that, for all his idealism, I, not he, was their truest friend.

I have enjoyed myself so much at the Oxford Union in later years that I am surprised, looking back, that I hardly ever spoke there as an undergraduate. Perhaps I was discouraged by the report in *Isis* of my maiden speech: 'Mr Pakenham rose like a ghost and like a ghost faded into the night.' I was an active member, however, of the small, select Conservative Club, the Canning. I can remember reading a paper on Parnell and concluding that he was 'a great Conservative'.

Very often on Sundays I would walk to Elsfield Manor, the home of John Buchan, under the tutorage, one might say, of Conservative pundits: Roger Makins, now Lord Sherfield; Alan Lennox-Boyd, later Lord Boyd; Wedderburn, later Lord Dundee; and Evelyn Baring, later Lord Harwich. The shortest of the four was Evelyn Baring who was over six foot three. I sometimes felt like Dreyfus being marched off to prison by four enormous cuirassiers.

I have met many kind people throughout my life and benefited greatly from their kindness, but no one was ever kinder than John Buchan, whose books I knew by heart. He once said to me, 'When you reach my age, Frank, you will realise that what people call snobbishness is nothing but a longing for romance.' His kindness was extended alike to dukes and sons of dustmen.

The two closest friends I made at New College were Evan Durbin and Hugh Gaitskell. Evan would certainly have become a cabinet minister in later years but he died helping a young child to safety off the Cornish coast. The phrase 'a genius for friendship' has been much overworked, but it might have been coined to describe Evan. It involved on his part unremitting activity on behalf of his friends, as I was to learn to my great benefit when I was defeated in the parliamentary elections in 1945.

Hugh Gaitskell and I were also close; we went into 'digs' together in 2 Isis Street in our third year. When he arrived at New College, Hugh was as conventional as I was an Etonian. By the beginning of the summer term, 1926, he had undergone something of a sea change, hinted at to me rather vaguely, the General Strike bringing to a head his concern for the working class. He chose the rather grim-sounding subject, Working-

Class Movements 1815–75, as his special subject in Modern Greats, and in his last years became an active member of the Socialist group run by G.D.H. Cole. Hugh read far more widely than I did: Proust and D.H. Lawrence for instance, stimulated by his cousin George Martelli who has been a dear friend to Elizabeth and me for sixty-five years or more. Hugh got a first after a viva, but in case I seemed to labour my superior performance, I would say that by the end of our time together he was the much more cultured man.

If I am asked, did I predict Hugh's subsequent greatness, I, like all his friends, I think, would have to admit that I didn't. He was popular with everyone, known to be an excellent golfer, but he was frankly unobtrusive. Years later when I heard his famous 'Fight, fight and fight again' speech at the Labour conference, I realised that, as John Strachey said of him, he had a 'will like a diving spear', and had developed true eloquence.

No one can say what kind of performance he would have put up as prime minister, which he certainly would have been if he had not died in 1963. He would have had to overcome a streak of intolerance, contempt for those who differed from him; but by the end of his life I felt that he was overcoming it. When I looked at an old television programme recently, he was speaking with a depth of feeling that nobody seems to reproduce nowadays. The words, 'He nothing common did or mean upon that memorable scene' come home to me whenever I think of him.

An older friend than any of these was Roger Chetwode, son of Field Marshal Chetwode, with whom I had 'messed' at Eton. He was the only schoolfriend who ever asked me to stay with him. His parents were then living at Government House, Aldershot. On the occasion of my visit George V and Queen Mary were coming to dinner. The house party was drawn up formally, waiting for Their Majesties. There was no sign of Roger. At the last minute he bustled in with the words, 'Sorry, Father, I forgot my medals.' Then and always he was forgiven much. He was unbelievably popular with everyone.

At Oxford he secured my election to the Bullingdon Club,

associated with hunting and aristocracy but open to agreeable, well-endowed Americans. No one but Roger could ever have secured my election. I had hardly known of the club's existence before, but once a member I joined in our common belief that we were the salt of the earth.

Roger went down after my third year, but two glamorous undergraduates arrived on the scene with a prolonged effect on my social life. One was Freddie (Viscount) Furneaux, son of the first Lord Birkenhead, the other Basil, son of the Marquess of Dufferin and Ava. In the next chapter I will say more about my life at the Birkenhead home. I will only mention now that Freddie eventually became my best man, and I acted as best man for Basil.

Basil was a Brackenbury scholar at Balliol, and the nearest approach to Byron that my generation could provide. He was, as his Eton tutor said of Rosebery, 'if not a poet, of the stuff that poets delighted'. John Betjeman, to whom he was much attached, wrote a poem for him after he was killed in the war.

> *and so you remained to me always*
> *Humorous, reckless, loyal –*
> *my kind, heavy-lidded companion.*
> *Stop, oh many bells, stop*
> *pouring on roses and creeper*
> *Your unremembering peal*
> *this hollow, unhallowed V.E. day –*
> *I am deaf to your notes and dead*
> *by a soldier's body in Burma.*

I was lucky to persuade Freddie and Basil to undertake the joint editorship of the *Oxford University Review,* a weekly paper I had started. Meanwhile, a certain Mr Sissons, the supposedly sinister owner of *Cherwell,* had secured the services of Bryan Guinness, later Lord Moyne, and Edward Hulton, both understood to be millionaires.

Bryan Moyne had been my exact contemporary in Wells House at Eton. When he died I was much honoured to deliver a memorial address about him in Trinity College Chapel in Dublin. My conclusion, that he had the sweetest nature of anyone I have every known, met with universal approval. Edward Hulton's greatest achievement was the establishment of *Picture Post*, which had a large influence in the war and immediately post-war period. There came a moment when Sissons invited me to call on him on the mysterious houseboat he lived in on the Thames. Ushering me in, he closed and put his back against the door. 'Look out, Pakenham,' he began. 'We can do some business if you have any sense in your head. You've got the names and I've got the money – what about a deal?' Somehow or other I escaped from the houseboat.

In those days undergraduates were, in theory, divided into Hearties and Aesthetes, although there was much overlapping and the majority would not have kept to either label. I was probably more of a Hearty that an Aesthete, although anxious to stand well with both. I enjoyed OUDS Smokers although I was hardly at home there. I can still see a young man squirming on the platform as he delivered the lines:

> *I'm just a jumper boy, my mother's only joy,*
> *I swear it's true.*
> *And when I do my tricks,*
> *With Joy or Helen Trix,*
> *I'm in an awful fix*
> *Because I only know the way*
> *To jump a boy.*

How far were the Aesthetes of that time practising homosexuals? No one, perhaps, will make a just assessment, least of all someone like myself who, as Dr Rowse has already been quoted as saying, 'has lacked homosexual experience'. The coming of the women has changed the whole scene beyond recognition.

27

4
SPORT

All my life, I have been addicted to sport, as a humble performer and an avid spectator. In my late eighties, I still put in four and a half miles on the road on Saturdays and Sundays, jogging much of the way *very* slowly. I have always loved sport, but I would be in every way a more civilised person if I had a better appreciation of good music.

A few years ago I made a despairing effort in that direction. I paid £2 for admittance to a local government course in musical appreciation. It was described reassuringly as 'for beginners only'. We sat around in a circle and our instructor asked each of us in turn to name our favourite record. Everyone mentioned one, some more than one. When it came to my turn, I spluttered helplessly: 'I am only here because I haven't got a favourite record.' Looks of contempt were universal. I slunk away resolved not to return till I had at least one favourite record.

I'm not altogether sure which is my favourite sport, either. At preparatory school, I won the half mile (our longest race) with consummate ease. During most of my time at Eton I was afflicted with flat feet which did not prevent me captaining the winning House football team as already mentioned, but ruled out competitive athletics. By the time I went to Oxford, however, I was running several miles on occasion with my uncle Arthur Villiers, an old Oxford three-mile Blue. I happened to

28

be staying at Eton when the school athletics master, by then middle-aged, was setting off for a run.

I happily joined him and we ran together for perhaps three miles. Suddenly he said to me, 'See what you can do.' I sprinted for home leaving him far behind, to his obvious pleasure. He at once asked me to run a half-mile for the old Etonians at the Queen's Club, in a relay team that included David Burleigh, soon to become an Olympic gold medallist. I went into violent training, too violent as it proved. Severe stomach pains led to a diagnosis of impending appendicitis. So my great opportunity was lost. The threat of appendicitis vanished; perhaps it was what is now called psychosomatic. But I kept up running for pleasure.

When I was a don at Christ Church, I used to run a mile and a quarter round Christ Church meadows every day between tutorials. When I was just on forty I ran a mile in just under five minutes at a sports meeting on the Iffley Road; nothing very notable to boast about, but many who have enjoyed running without being champions will know what I mean.

I did not play rugger at Eton, and played it only intermittently at Oxford. I did participate, however, on one quite notable occasion. I went down with a scratch fifteen to play against Harrow in the first rugby football match in their history. One of our team, a liability as it turned out, was a famous Irish rugby international called Stuart who was coaching Harrow, and was determined that they should win their first game. We were leading by two points with a few minutes to go, but Stuart was not to be thwarted. Lurking persistently offside he at last caused the referee – the famous Potter Irwin – to penalise him. 'Caught me that time, Potter old man,' said Stuart chuckling immoderately. The Harrovian captain duly kicked a penalty goal, so honour was more or less satisfied all round.

When the Eton Manor Club in Hackney Wick took up rugger I played for them in their first game, but my opportunities did not really occur till Elizabeth and I lived near Aylesbury, where my mother had a cottage to spare, soon after we married. Aylesbury was also starting up rugger. I played for them at what would now be called number 8, but was then middle of the back row when one packed 323 instead of 341, as now. It seems unlikely, but I scored a try in every match that season and was duly elected captain for the next year.

I obtained recruits of the utmost value from Oxford in Dick Crossman and Patrick Gordon Walker; dons and, more to the point, previous Greyhounds (University second XV). I was not so successful when my great friend Eleanor Smith contributed someone whom she described as having been a Romanian international. Unfortunately he had been a boxing champion and had little idea of the rules of rugby football. When challenged by the referee for picking the ball out of the scrum he turned round and laid him out. I will draw a veil over what occurred next.

I was invited to play for Buckinghamshire, by no means then what they are now, but urgent academic business prevented me from accepting. So once again my sporting aspirations remained unfulfilled.

While on the subject of football, this time soccer, I shall tax the credulity of readers by saying that at the age of sixty-six in 1972 I played soccer against Bobby Moore, hero of the 1966 world championship and so much else. I was induced by Jon Snow, now a national figure, then co-ordinator of the New Horizon Youth Centre, to play in a charity match.

As we changed in the dressing room, Bobby Moore put me at my ease by remarking, 'You look pretty fit.' I could only return the compliment. I would certainly not have dared to call him Bobby.

As the game proceeded I found myself continually being robbed of the ball by Moore, but he has often been referred to as 'the great gentleman of sport', and certainly his handling of me was exquisitely gentle. The outcome was rather sad. Instead of being photographed arm-in-arm with Bobby Moore I appeared in the tabloids with a couple of Bunny Girls who had somehow inserted themselves into the scene and snuggled up all too close to me.

Looking back, I seem to have spent an extraordinary number of hours playing tennis. At our family home in Westmeath, my sister Mary and I played endlessly on a very soft court, on which I developed a most unattractive type of cut shot. We played a lot of croquet, too, and table tennis, then called ping pong. Many years later I played several years running in the County Cavan tennis tournament. One year, the local potentate, Lord Farnham, and I got into the final of the men's doubles assisted by the terror which he generated among our local opponents. A couple of Irish Davis Cup players descended on us from Dublin who seemed to know nothing of Lord Farnham and still less of myself. They walloped us in the final. As we left the court I said to Lord Farnham, 'I'm afraid I let you down.' He replied tolerantly, 'Can't keep going all the time.'

When I taught at Oxford, 1932–9, I played tennis almost every afternoon on the Iffley Road courts. I once reached the semi-final of the *Oxford Mail* championship, but was defeated in 'straight sets' by the county champion. I beat him a few days later in a friendly match but my self-esteem was soon diminished. I then played against the number two in the county, expecting to win. As time passed I realised something was seriously amiss. To put it crudely, I wasn't winning any points at all. Twenty-four points can go by all too quickly. At the end of the set, as we crossed over, he obviously expected some comment from me on this total whitewash. I could only mutter, 'Let's get on with it.' I came close to winning the next two sets, but pride that day had a nasty fall – not for the last time.

I have had enormous pleasure out of golf. For thirty years I played every weekend at Rye, at the club to which I was introduced by my old cricket captain, G.O. (Gubby) Allen. I once won the monthly medal from a handicap of 15, but in those days I used to putt effectively between my legs. When the rules were altered and they banned this procedure, I deteriorated to 18. I won many matches on that handicap because a vast number of weekend golfers liked to call themselves 18 when 28 was nearer the mark.

Two of the golfing four in which I joined died on the links, in one case in the professional's shop. The fourth, Henry Burrows, left the neighbourhood and died soon afterwards. He was Assistant Clerk in the House of Lords and was very unfairly treated in not being made Clerk of Parliament. When

I was Leader of the House of Lords I persuaded the cabinet to adopt what was really his plan for reforming the House, under which hereditary peers would have been allowed to continue to speak in the House but not to vote. Henry called it the Two-Writ plan. Henry and I had many enjoyable times together. Only once did I falter in friendship. I had just missed a putt and he had just holed one on the windswept seventh green. As we made our way down to the plain he turned to me and said, by no means for the first time: 'You do believe in the Two-Writ plan don't you?' But that was the only time when I did not delight in Henry's company.

I have already written about my cricket-playing at Eton, and my friendship with G.O. (Gubby) Allen. Many years later, I came to know Douglas Jardine quite well. He used to come down to the Eton Manor Club, presided over by my uncle, and coach the boys indefatigably at cricket. One evening he, by this time Captain of the England Cricket XI, brought Harold Larwood, the great fast bowler, to dinner at 'The Manor'. They were just setting off for the famous, or notorious, tour in Australia, later called the Bodyline tour. Jardine demonstrated on the dinner table exactly how Bodyline would work. It was all done in his best Wykehamist manner without any hint that anyone would get hurt. There was no doubt, however, that he was determined to bring Bradman to book by any means in his power.

In the event, Larwood practised Bodyline under Jardine's instruction to a point where Commonwealth relations were threatened. Gubby Allen refused to bowl it, true to the highest traditions of our cricketing House, where we were commanded to win – but not quite at all costs.

My love of cricket, vicarious cricket at any rate, has never left me. I have had the honour, with the help of Major Horsfall, at the House of Lords, to have entertained at lunch Keith Miller, Dennis Compton and the Bedser brothers. I am in the happy position of being able to tell them of how I saw Gregory McDonald bowling at the Oval in 1921, of England inspired by Hobbs and Rhodes recovering the Ashes in 1926, and above all Bradman scoring 254 at Lord's in 1930. I have for many years now been President of the Hurst Green Cricket Club. Until fairly recently (though it's probably longer ago than I care to think) I turned out against the village once a year, with a team brought by Geoffrey Coppinger, formerly of the National Bank and a supreme authority on the recent history of cricket.

I used to station myself at mid-on, on the theory that no catches would come my way in that position, and for a number of years none ever did. But one day there was a high wind. The ball started as usual in the direction of mid-off, but flew round towards me. It seemed to circle around me as I gradually collapsed under it. Finally it landed on my prostrate body. I claimed a catch, but it was not awarded and I never turned out again.

My son-in-law Harold Pinter is a passionate lover of cricket. He has taken his team round the country for the last twenty years, and brought it regularly to play against Hurst Green. It is an additional bond of friendship between us.

I also retain my passion for vicarious rugby. I have been to Twickenham times without number, and often to Lansdowne Road, Cardiff Arms Park, Murrayfield and the Parc des Princes, in Paris. I was at Twickenham in 1925 when one of the Brownlies of the New Zealand team was sent off; I cheered for Ireland, as I have said, when I was in the British cabinet. I have learned far more about the detail of the game when watching on television, with the benefit of expert commentary, but there is nothing to compare with being present at a match. That is, if your side wins. Otherwise, it is better to suffer in solitude at home.

I should say a word about my horsemanship, or lack of it. My father was a master of the Westmeath Hounds, so we grew up in an atmosphere of horses – in our case, ponies. With my father's death, however, that more or less came to an end.

I had, therefore, ridden very little when, in 1928, I competed in the Bullingdon Grind point-to-point (a countryside steeplechase for amateurs). I hired a horse from Mac, the Oxford horse dealer, for 30 shillings, and found myself competing against my friend Bill, later Viscount Astor, who was mounted on a horse called Geoffrey Austin, understood to be worth £2,000 (£50,000+ today). I careered over the first fence but was bowled over by an equally incompetent rider and lost my crash helmet. I remounted and made my way to the tenth fence, where I came completely unstuck, getting a bump on the head which caused concussion. When I came to, some facetious onlookers had pointed my horse in the wrong direction, and called out, 'That's the way!' I jumped the fence backwards and made good progress until I encountered the only surviving jockey, Bill Astor, on the aforesaid Geoffrey Austin, who did not welcome my intervention. I took up the refrain, 'That's the way!' trying to dissuade him from pursuing a winning course. He managed to evade me and eventually I was brought under control.

I had enormously enjoyed the training sessions before the race, and after going down from Oxford actually bought a horse worth £130. I did a year's hunting under the tutelage of the famous farmer and horseman Bletsoe who had ridden over the Grand National course. But my riding lapsed until many years later when I was staying at what is now Tullynally Castle in Westmeath, as my son's guest. The talk turned on hunting and I found myself expressing regret that there was no horse available for me on which to participate in the Boxing Day meet the next day. I was informed at once that one could be quickly obtained, as could the necessary kit. The horse in question, Salome, was said to be an excellent jumper but to dislike water.

Next day I set off full of nervous resolution, and was unpleasantly surprised that the first obstacle was a brook. Salome stopped short; I assumed this was a refusal and, as it were, prepared to move backward for another attempt. Salome jumped the brook, leaving me prostrate on the ground, which was mercifully soft.

Next day the *Westmeath Examiner* reported, 'Lord Longford took a toss early but gallantly remounted and stayed with hounds all day – a good performance.' I only stayed with hounds in the sense that when they checked at the innumerable banks I rejoined them before they moved on, and at the finish there I was, up with the leaders. It at least enables me to make better conversation with hunting people than with racing motorists.

Antonia has asked me whether I couldn't say something about

the value of sport in the formation of character. I have no doubt in my mind that sports like cricket and football are capable of producing a team spirit which, as far as it goes, is a form of selflessness. On the other hand, cricket – for those who have no gift for ball games, and football – for those who are physically frail, can be a nightmare. This seems to be more widely recognised today than when I was young.

At Eton there was, admittedly, the possibility of opting out of cricket; one could become a 'wet bob' (as opposed to a dry bob). In our House this was rare. In my recollection, only four boys in all the time I was at Wells' became wet bobs. One of them was my brother, another was Reggie Manningham-Buller, later Lord Dilhorne. Reggie, gauche and bespectacled (which I should have been but wasn't at that time), was mocked for his activities on the river. When he went in for a race we used to go down with megaphones and shout, 'Out, Buller, out,' which once ran him into a passing steamer. When he recovered, we took up the cry of 'In, Buller, in', which took him into the bank. But years later at a House dinner of old boys we positively fawned on Reggie – by then Lord Chancellor, even more than Gubby Allen, who had by then captained England at cricket. So Reggie, whose son is a welcome addition to the House of Lords, had the last laugh after all.

I cannot exaggerate my own dedication to the cause of winning the House football cup. I was captain of our under-fourteen-and-a-half team when we were defeated in the final. H.V. McNaughton, a dear old sentimentalist, later Provost, came up to me and patted me on the head saying, 'The spirit of the ancient Gweeks, little boy.' Much later he told me that 'little boy' was the most beautiful phrase in the English language, but the Latin 'puerulus' was even more beautiful. For years I cherished the dream of captaining the winning House team. I cared far more for that than for any possible achievement of my own. When I led in our winning team Basil Dufferin always insisted that I was roundly hissed, but I was oblivious of that at the time, if indeed it occurred.

However, to be a dedicated captain is more understandable than to be an equally dedicated member of the rank and file. While I was writing this Harold (Pinter) told me with shining eyes that two members of his cricket team, the Gaiety, had made 264 runs for the first wicket. I couldn't help saying, 'How awful for the rest of the team.' He thought that was a feeble comment. The rest of the team were overjoyed and gave the two heroes a dinner. In other words, they cared so much for the success of the Gaiety that they felt no sadness at not having had an innings themselves.

As for the character-forming potential of individual sports – let us take athletics as an example. The story of Linford Christie is surely inspiring to the rest of us as we jog away in our eighties.

5
THE FIRST
LORD BIRKENHEAD
AND CHARLTON

In April 1928 Freddie (Viscount) Furneaux, later the second Lord Birkenhead, took me over to his family home, Charlton, about twenty-two miles from Oxford. When I arrived, Margaret Birkenhead, his mother, her dark eyes always shining with humour, said to me, 'Do you know my girls?' The two young women were seated on a sofa with their backs to me; Eleanor perhaps twenty-five, Pam around fourteen. Eleanor extended her arm backwards for me to shake. Pam followed her example.

I was now a fully-fledged member of the Charlton circle. The first Lord Birkenhead (F.E. Smith as he will be remembered in the history books) loomed up, a massive presence. If I had been told that he had been heavyweight boxing champion of England thirty years earlier (he was fifty-six at this time), I would have believed it.

'Do you ride?' he asked. My most recent experience of horsemanship was coming unstuck at the Bullingdon point-to-point. I was dressed in grey flannels, but this was apparently no objection. The Birker, as we young people came to call him, offered me a piece of string to tie them up. He did likewise with his own trousers.

We set off – he on an enormous black charger, I on a white polo pony whose mouth had acquired a hardness from many international championships. Soon we were both out of control in a neighbouring field. My fear of imminent death was obliterated in a greater terror as Lord Birkenhead drew alongside me on the mighty black, cursing vociferously but as utterly helpless as I was. Round and round the field we tore until finally and for no obvious reason the white pony lost interest, the black mercifully followed suit, and both came to a stop with their noses pointing towards home.

We jogged back in silence. Apart from one visit to Roger Chetwode, this was my first venture outside my family, and it seemed likely to end on the same evening it began. When we reached the house, Lord Birkenhead turned to me.

'We have survived,' he said, 'though you will not, I feel sure, claim an undue share of credit for our achievement. We have preserved our skins, if not our dignity. In reciting these events to the ladies it would be unwise and, indeed, injudicious to depress their spirits and our own prestige with too slavish an adherence to the literal facts as they may have appeared at the moment of their occurrence.'

He shot me the rich, warm, illuminating smile of partnership that I came to know so well, and went in to pitch some tremendous yarn in which he and I won infinite glory and saved each other's lives.

It is not easy to convey in writing the magic of Lord Birkenhead's personality as it imposed itself on young undergraduates like myself. I remember him once beginning an after-dinner speech (he was a master of the art) by saying that he proposed to dwell equally on 'the grave and the gay'. In a sense his life, as it appeared to us, was a combination of the two (this was long before the word 'gay' acquired its present connotation).

His oratory, which I experienced on only one occasion in the Oxford Union, was magnificent. I will quote only one specimen, drawn from a speech in which he was setting out to promote peace in Ireland. (Ireland he described as that island of incomparable beauty, so individual in her genius, so tenacious in love and hate, so captivating in her nobler moods.) That was the grave; for an example of the gay, I will turn to his dialogue with an elderly hairdresser in Oxford. I was in the next chair when I heard the barber say to him, 'Not quite so thick as usual, m'lord.' F.E. prided himself, justifiably, on his thick black locks. He turned round and noticed that the ancient hairdresser was completely bald. 'You're not so hot yourself, are you?' he observed.

When he died, his great friend Winston Churchill paid a worthy tribute to him, but it contained the words 'he was always great fun'. This irritated the family, who thought it trivialised their mighty father, but in fact he was a fun man incarnate, as well as having many more impressive qualities.

Playing golf with him of a morning, or an afternoon game of tennis before tea (with riding to follow), I was, as were all my contemporaries, perpetually amused. Over sixty years later I made what in all modesty was a very successful speech at a big Irish dinner in the Dorchester. Tony O'Reilly, supreme rugby football international and now a super-tycoon, applauded it with the words, 'Come back, Harold Macmillan.' I was pleased, but I would have been still more excited if he had said 'Come back F.E. Smith.'

Macmillan, considered a bore in his younger days, had admittedly become a spellbinder by the time he reached the House of Lords at the age of ninety, but in his case it was a tremendous theatrical effect. With F.E., the wit and humour flowed out incessantly. He had the supreme and very unusual quality in a distinguished man of revelling in the company of the young, particularly the young from Oxford, to which he was always devoted. He was High Steward of the university but never, alas, Chancellor. John Buchan, later Lord Tweedsmuir, a kind patron of mine for a number of years, told me that when it fell to him to inform F.E. that he could not be Chancellor, the latter urbanely replied, 'What Oxford requires at this crisis of her fortunes, my dear John, is a decorous façade. That, unfortunately, I am unable to provide.'

No one can conceal the fact that his death at the age of fifty-eight was precipitated by his heavy drinking, but I never saw that side of him in the many weekends I spent at Charlton. His family life was delightful, there is no other word. Margaret Birkenhead was the daughter of a famous scholar, referred to by F.E. as a 'Tacitean scholar so formidable that even Tacitus would have hesitated to do battle with him'. 'The Birker' was proud of her old family, which included Joseph Severn, the intimate friend of Keats. When F.E. died, Seymour Berry, eldest son of Lord Camrose and an active member of the Charlton set, asked me to write something about him for the *Sunday Times.* I produced a glowing piece which ended with the words, 'When one thinks of the great and generous heart, one thinks first and last of the love he bore for his wife.' The editor of the *Sunday Times* viewed me with infinite cynicism, commenting, 'No one will swallow that; why don't you write about him as a hero of Oxford undergraduates?' However, I stuck to my point and the piece duly appeared. Margaret Birkenhead wrote to thank me and told me, which I always accepted, that theirs had been a very happy marriage.

Freddie Furneaux was Keeper of the Field (captain of the football team) at Eton, and a tennis Blue, both achievements which meant a lot to his father. He had the dark saturnine looks of the latter but his mother's acute sensitivity. He went on to produce a fine series of biographies including two books about his father. When I delivered an address at his memorial service at Westminster, R.A. Butler, who had become a close friend of Freddie's in later years, said to me in his well-known ambiguous style, 'Very good of course, but I was at the front. It's a pity they don't put in microphones here, but I could hear perfectly.'

Eleanor became a best-selling romantic novelist and eventually a Roman Catholic. Pam, beautiful both as a girl and as a mature woman, has frequently been described as a leading Society hostess, but neither she nor any of her family would have been happy with such as assessment. Her marriage to Michael Berry, younger son of Lord Camrose, was as happy as Freddie's to Sheila, Michael's elder sister. She is credited with having played a large part in the success of the *Telegraph* newspapers during her lifetime.

If I am asked what influence this glamorous family exercised on me, I find it impossible to answer. Certainly not in any straightforward way was I affected by the views of Birkenhead, who would now be called a right-wing Conservative. Nor was my movement to the Catholic Church influenced by the Charlton circle, but I would have said that there was a lot of sympathy there, not only because of Eleanor's conversion. Father Martin D'Arcy, the Jesuit who became my guru, was very friendly with Freddie. Margaret Birkenhead's father had been a clergyman after his retirement from his professorship at Oxford. Indeed, he had become Vicar of Aynho, very close to my mother's home at Middleton Park. My mother and Margaret Birkenhead had been close friends in childhood. The latter was the first to understand my need for spiritual certainty.

In his younger days, F.E. had been a yeomanry officer with the Oxfordshire, Bucks and Berks when my father had commanded the militia. My uncle Arthur Villiers had served alongside him. When I first met him, F.E. said to me, 'Your father did not altogether approve of me but I am very happy to meet his son.' In the end, I cannot trace direct effects resulting from my friendship over many years with this family. But then and always they enhanced my self-esteem and provided a friendship that has never faltered.

6
THE YOUNG SOCIALITE

In the years after leaving Oxford I became an occasional visitor at one grand house and a regular visitor at another. The first house was Taplow Court, home of Lord and Lady Desborough, where the traditions of the 'Souls' were maintained in top-flight aristocratic culture. The second was Cliveden, home of Lord and Lady Astor, where high politics were mixed up with social interests and where a younger generation figured prominently.

I came to stay at Taplow almost by chance. Moggie (Imogen), the unmarried daughter of the house, who later married George (Viscount) Gage with whom she made an immensely popular couple, rang me up at short notice and asked me to make up the numbers. When I arrived on a Saturday afternoon I found that the number I in fact made up was thirteen, so it was obvious that I should take myself off as soon as possible.

The house party, if on the elderly side by my standards, was high-powered. Winston and Clementine Churchill, Duff and Diana Cooper, Lord D'Abernon, the former ambassador in Germany and elsewhere, were typical. Unfortunately from my point of view, Sir Maurice (Bongie) Bonham Carter, husband of Violet, the finest woman orator of her generation, had also been roped in. No one was unkind to me, but I was a very small fish in this glamorous pond. After-dinner guessing games were played. Everyone had to retire in turn. Finally it fell to my lot. When I came back to the drawing room the house party excelled themselves in flights of fancy. 'I think she reminds me of a peach melba,' said one. 'Yes', said another, 'but don't you see a sprig of mistletoe inserted?' I gazed at them in gauche bewilderment. The women both started shrieking at me, 'Oh but you must see who it is!' I looked more befuddled than ever. Finally they revealed the name. 'It's Barbara!' they cried. 'You *must* see it's Barbara!' I had never heard of Barbara and cannot now remember who she was. But I escaped next morning as soon as possible.

Cliveden was totally different, though geographically close at hand in the Thames Valley. I originally met Lord Astor under rather unfortunate circumstances. You will remember that it was his son Bill, on a valuable horse, with whom I almost collided at the Bullingdon point-to-point. Bill had selected me to introduce to his father that very evening, as the most promising young man of his generation whom he could recommend for the *Observer*, owned by the Astors then and for many years afterwards. I am afraid that Lord Astor cannot have obtained a very favourable idea of Bill's generation if this young fellow – heavily concussed, I should mention – was the best that would be exhibited. With his unfailing charm he questioned me about my views on the future of the House of Lords but I could do nothing but goggle and giggle. What might have been a great career in journalism was denied me.

But Waldorf Astor was a very forgiving man. Soon afterwards I was invited to stay at Cliveden and went down with him to Eton to see his second son, David, running in the hurdles. David won at a canter, joining Waldorf Astor and me with the same diffident smile on his face which he sustained throughout the years in the midst of great journalistic and social achievements.

Until recently, my oldest friend was Aidan Crawley, the most glamorous member of the Bullington in my time. An international cricketer who, I always heard, scored more runs in the Parks than anyone before or since. Aidan was soon selected to be the twelfth man for the England Cricket XI. I have also often heard, but he denied this, that when called on as a replacement, he took the field at Lord's in tennis shoes and was sharply criticised by the older members. Be that as it may, I have little doubt that he would have gone on not only to play for England for many years, but to captain the England XI, if he had not decided to pursue a career in journalism.

Aidan has always been my model of an idealist; he obtained a Labour Party candidature (to the surprise of all his friends, but I am glad to think assisted by me) just before the war. He was a daring fighter pilot, shot down and imprisoned in Germany for several years. I have been told, for example by the present Lord Barber, who shared his prison experiences, that Aidan was the life and soul of the camp. He was engaged in many attempted escapes and once made his way to the frontier. After the war, he won North Bucks for Labour, became an Under-Secretary for Air, and would undoubtedly have gone far in the party. He was exactly the kind of Labour MP who appealed to Clem Attlee.

He lost his marginal seat in 1951, one view being that my final address calling for sacrifices in the name of religion was the decisive debit. He then had a very successful career in television, then reappeared in the House of Commons – as a Conservative; still idealistic, still a great friend of mine, whatever our views of the moment.

The word glamour inevitably attaches itself to all the Crawleys, but also, alas, all too much tragedy in recent years. Virginia, his magnetic wife, war correspondent and author, much loved by Elizabeth and me, was killed in a car accident in which Aidan was seriously injured. His two sons, possessed of all the Crawley games-playing ability, style and daring, were killed flying. Through it all, Aidan remained indomitable and cheerful, as one knew all along that he would. His daughter, Harriet, is a special favourite of all my family. Sadly, she has not yet obtained the seat in parliament which we all agree she deserves.

David Astor is now my oldest friend. I pause to offer a few thoughts about someone who has done so much good and at all times 'blushed to find fame'. During the twenty-seven years when he was editor of the *Observer*, the paper emanated a high-mindedness which reflected his own personality. When I first knew him, his guru was Tom Jones (TJ), private secretary to Lloyd George, Bonar Law and Baldwin. Later the Reverend Michael Scott, champion of human rights in South Africa, was central in David's life. Later again, Peter Timms, former governor of Maidstone Prison, now the Reverend Peter Timms, Methodist minister, was associated with David in every aspect of penal reform.

David has played a large part in my life, acting as my social conscience. When I became Minister for Germany, he inspired an article in the *Observer* which said of me, 'If he fails, he will confess to failure, and if impeded, he will resign.' I never forgot those words even if I did not live up to them at the time. I did not resign over Germany, though I made more than one attempt to. I have no doubt that my resignation in 1968 from Harold Wilson's cabinet was the ultimate fruit of David's confidence in my integrity.

I cannot believe there are any house parties today like those at Cliveden in the thirties. Prime ministers, ambassadors, rising politicians like Anthony Eden when he became Foreign Secretary, rubbed shoulders with social workers from Plymouth, which Nancy Astor represented in parliament, and Christian Scientists – also constituents, otherwise somewhat inexplicable. Nancy Astor, indeed, took me to the Christian Science church in Maidenhead, presumably as a potential recruit. She forgave me readily enough when I became a Socialist later, but never, I am afraid, quite got over my becoming a Roman Catholic. On that issue there is no denying that she and Waldorf, both deeply religious in their way, were bigoted. In those days a policy, long since reversed, was followed of not allowing Jews or Catholics to occupy responsible positions on the *Observer*.

I have never at any time encountered discussions like the ones at Cliveden after dinner, the ladies having withdrawn (these often included Joyce Grenfell, Nancy's niece, who became the world-famous comedienne). The seniors congregated at one end of the table; the juniors, Bill's friends such as myself, at another. Nevertheless, sometimes one found oneself talking to a man of the hour. In 1930 Tom (Sir Oswald)

Mosley, then aged thirty-four, had just resigned from the Labour government. Everyone was all over him, including rising Conservatives like Harold Macmillan and Bob Boothby. Women whispered that he had some secret drug that gave him supernatural potency.

I remember asking him diffidently about the future of political leadership. He spoke with total confidence. 'After Peel comes Disraeli. After Baldwin and MacDonald comes –' he looked to me to supply the obvious answer. I hesitated. He went on rather sharply, 'Well, comes someone very different.'

At the top of the table one could hear J.L. Garvin, *Observer* editor for many years, booming away. 'When I was a boy there was a thing called duty. There was a thing called sense of shame. Those things are dead today. And now we have Phil Scott [the British heavyweight champion] lying down before that young American stripling, and we say the English know how to take a beating. In my younger days we did not take a beating.' With tremendous emphasis: 'We made sure it was the other fellow took a beating.'

Somebody piped up, 'Aren't you rather a pessimist, Mr Garvin?' Garvin submerged the questioner with a gesture. 'Pessimism and optimism, I'm above all isms. I'm above all that.' It was all very exciting for a young man in his early twenties. But no one looking at David Astor's dedicated service during the last half century can doubt that there was a social inspiration at work in Cliveden, as perhaps in no other house of the time.

I found inspiration also, however, at Hatfield, the home of the Salisburys. I was taken there by (Lord) David Cecil who became one of Elizabeth's and my greatest friends. Cecil was the most inspiring conversationalist I have ever known, and a supremely successful Oxford teacher. At Hatfield the atmosphere was one of deep Anglican tradition, with prayers in the house night and morning. When I reached the House of Lords many years later, the eldest son, Bobbety, dominated the scene. Labour were in power and we had only a handful of Labour peers. We were in one sense at the mercy of the multitude of Tories, although it would have been a very false move from their point of view if they had abused their position.

Bobbety set out to create the atmosphere of friendliness surpassing all Party differences, which has distinguished the House of Lords ever since.

An anecdote must be told to round off that compliment. A much esteemed member of the Labour Party in the House, Reg Wells Pestell, made some comment about the failure of Tory peers to declare their financial interest in Rhodesia, which caused great offence. Bobbety Salisbury was not present at the time, but the remarks might have been taken to apply to him in particular. The affronted Tory peers staged a sort of walk-out. Peter Carrington, Leader of the Opposition, came to me and told me that Wells Pestell would be *persona non grata* among the predominant Tories for some time. But Bobbety met Reg in the corridor and said to him, 'I gather that some of our fellows were upset by something you said the other day. But if that is what you felt, you were quite right to say it. This is not a club, it is a House of Parliament.' Reg told me the story with tears in his eyes.

To return to the Astors. In 1929 I spent three weeks staying with them in Plymouth, rendering some small assistance to Nancy in her campaign. She was a flaming orator, and insisted on the audience providing a reaction. I can hear her now denouncing them for being so passive, until at last she had created a real hubbub. Waldorf provided the perfect antidote. He told me that the secret was to bring a book on railway rates and read it to them. After a while they dozed off. I received unlimited kindness from both of them.

By the time that the Cliveden set was identified with a policy of appeasement with Germany, I was a young married Socialist, and though Elizabeth and I were made very welcome at Cliveden, I was much less intimate there.

In the sixties there was the sad story which led to Jack Profumo's resignation from his position of Secretary of State for War and the House of Commons. It led to the suicide of Stephen Ward who, as Bill Astor's osteopath, had a house in Cliveden's grounds, and to an unpleasant attitude towards Bill himself among many of his so-called friends. Looking back I am rather amazed to find that when Stephen Ward died I, who had barely met him, made my way on to television, and posed the question, standing by his grave, 'Which of us can cast the first stone?' I am glad to have done it. The other characters in the story all emerge in noble light. Bill died a deeply religious man. His beautiful wife Bron, now my friend of many years and a devout Catholic, has won a high reputation as a psychotherapist. Jack Profumo, supported at all times by Valerie, his beautiful wife, and by New Horizon, has devoted his life to work among the poor in East London, in the spirit of Clem Attlee in the years before 1914. It is altogether appropriate that it was Jack Profumo who took the initiative in the establishment of the Attlee Foundation.

7
SEEKING A ROLE
1928–32

When my grandchildren or other young graduates seem uncertain about what kind of job to seek or ambition to fulfil, I recall my own four years of uncertainty between leaving Oxford in 1928 and returning as a lecturer in 1932.

Much of my social life centred upon the Birkenhead family. The facts of my occupation, or lack of it, can be briefly stated. The concussion I had sustained in that unlucky race in spring 1928 gave me a kind of excuse for not genuinely seeking work immediately. I certainly cherished vague political aspirations, always of a Conservative character, but I was hoping to equip myself for a political role by becoming a professional economist.

That dream was shattered – in my own interests, as it proved – by a conversation with J.M. Keynes in the office of the stockbrokers Buckmaster & Moore in the summer of 1929. I had started work there just before the great slump of that year, and in the general enthusiasm of the time, I bought a share called Radio Corporation at $109 – I was shown a chart extrapolating its progress to at least $300. In the event, I sold out at $41, and was relieved when I noticed later that it had dropped to $5.

This misfortune, however, was irrelevant to my discussion with Keynes. He was already enormously admired in intellectual circles, although distrusted by such as the Governor of the

Bank of England. As a non-executive partner in the firm, he was kind enough to interview me, with a view to my undertaking research at Cambridge. I can still see him leaning across the table, his eyes boring into mine as he expressed his ideas. 'My trouble is', he said, 'that I cannot see into your mind.' I had the uneasy feeling that he could see into it all too effectively. 'At Cambridge we believe that we are a few years ahead of the rest of the world – maybe ten – twenty – maybe fifty years. I cannot tell whether you can go our pace, whether you can keep up.' He left me in no doubt that he was sure I could not. I was saved from a career for which my talent was limited.

A lucky break, however, came my way in the late summer of 1929. Through the good offices of Sandy (Lord) Lindsay, Master of Balliol, who had examined me at school, I was appointed a Workers' Educational Association tutor. I was to take classes in adult education in Fenton and Longton (Stoke-on-Trent). In Fenton I lived for part of the week in a working-class home; something I have never done before or since. I came away with a great sense of the untapped intellectual possibilities of working people.

This did not, however, prevent me accepting with equal alacrity a post in the Conservative Research Department, while I continued to make the journey once a week to the Potteries. Our chairman was Neville Chamberlain, who became Chancellor of the Exchequer halfway through my two-year stint in the Research Department. Elizabeth's mother, one of the Birmingham Chamberlains, was his first cousin, but that did not bias him in my favour. When we got married in November, 1931, his daughter Dorothy was one of the bridesmaids. The staff of the Research Department were invited to the wedding with their spouses or fiancés, but were required to return to the office before the reception, leaving their spouses or fiancés behind.

Only once did Chamberlain visit our department at 24 Old Queen Street, on the third floor overlooking St James's Park. And only once was I summoned to his presence. I had written a paper arguing that the Conservative Party were neglecting the Workers' Educational Association. I told the story of how I had attempted to obtain a post with the Association in London and had made the mistake of writing on Carlton Club writing paper. A female don (later my dear friend Lady Wootton) received me with the derisive words, 'What writing paper on which to apply for a job with the WEA!' Unfortunately, or otherwise, she was described in the typescript as 'a female dog'. I don't know to this day whether Neville Chamberlain realised that it was a misprint, but he was laughing when I came into the room, and he was still laughing when I left.

One of my seniors was Henry Brooke, later Home Secretary, the father of the present Heritage Minister. When I met the latter, I told him the word 'upright' was the word I always connected with his father, and he did not seem to feel that it was inappropriate.

The other senior, considerably older than Henry and myself, was Harold Stannard. He had many reminiscences of the Conservative Party in the old days. He had been a brilliant student at St Edward's, Birmingham, from which he had obtained a scholarship to Magdalen College, Oxford. When Neville Chamberlain visited Magdalen, the well-meaning President was anxious to present this young protégé from Birmingham to the great man, but Stannard told me that he shrank back; it was too much like meeting God. 'I told the President I preferred not to meet Mr Chamberlain.'

By 1930, his career had not amounted to much, but he retained an academic wit which Henry and I found very agreeable. Chamberlain, on the one occasion he did visit us, found himself at a loss for anything to say. He gazed across St James's Park and posed the question, 'I wonder if those trees are cherry trees?' Little Stannard, in his finest academic drawl, replied, 'All trees are cherry trees.' Chamberlain, clearly puzzled but anxious to be courteous to his staff, asked him, 'Surely that is rather an exaggeration?' Stannard knew the answer to that one: 'All truth is an exaggeration.' Perhaps that is why Chamberlain never visited our room again.

Mr Baldwin was kind to me on the few occasions we met, but I only once had the opportunity of a private talk with him. I was staying in a great country house and, to my immense surprise – for Mr Baldwin was supposed to be uninterested in

51

young politicians – I was informed by my hostess after lunch on Sunday that the great man would like me to go for a walk with him. (I have often wondered since whether he was conscious of having expressed any such desire, or whether it was my hostess who was anxious, as I am sure she was, to help me.)

I am ready to believe that with a better naturalist or more articulate lover of the countryside, Mr Baldwin would have found it easier to converse freely and gaily. As it was, the conversation lagged painfully. Only once, when I mentioned his son Oliver, did Mr Baldwin brighten. 'Dear fellow,' he exclaimed, coming to life suddenly. Then we trudged on again in virtual silence. Finally, as the house came in sight, I grew desperate. Somehow I must find out a little of the profound political philosophy with which I unquestioningly credited my leader. I informed him that I was teaching political theory for the WEA in the Potteries, and asked him, in full naïvety and with no shadow of irony, which were the political thinkers to whom he himself owed most.

He reflected for a moment and then spoke quietly and emphatically to this effect: 'There is one political thinker who has had more influence on me than all others – Sir Henry Maine. When I was at Cambridge, his authority was complete and I never ceased to be grateful for all I learnt from him.' I was of course all ears. After all, the walk had been anything but vain.

'What', I persisted, as innocently as before, 'would you say was Maine's supreme contribution?' Mr Baldwin paused perhaps a shade longer and then said with conviction: 'Rousseau argued that all human progress was from contract to status, but Maine made it clear once and for all that the real movement was from status to contract.' He paused again, this time for quite a while, and suddenly a look of dawning horror, but at the same time of immense humanity and confederacy stole across his face. 'Or was it,' he said, leaning just a little towards me, 'or was it the other way round?'

The crucial event in these interim years, the event that determined my future, was a visit I paid to Oxford in the summer of 1930, as the result of a dream. It sounds almost like one of those dreams in the New Testament, where Joseph is told to 'take your wife and young child into Egypt'. The message that came to me in my dream was: 'Call on Elizabeth at 10 Chadlington Road, Oxford.'

A little recapitulation is now required. I never met a female undergraduate during my time at Oxford until the Commemoration Ball at New College in 1927, after I had taken my final 'schools' exams. I had fallen asleep in the rooms taken by Hugh Gaitskell in the Great Quad, New College, at about 3 AM. I awoke to find a beautiful vision bending over me. Sixty-five years later, I can fairly call it love at first sight.

But a long interval followed. Elizabeth remained at Oxford for another three years, to occupy a position that perhaps no woman student ever occupied before or since; to become the first woman *Isis* idol was only one of her triumphs. Today, when nearly half the students are women, such an individual pre-eminence would be impossible.

By 1930 she was at the centre of a number of circles. The one that excited her most was that presided over by the famous scholar and wit Maurice Bowra, then Dean of Wadham. Elizabeth, as usual, describes his appearance much better than I can. ' . . . Tiny feet and short legs apart, miraculously supporting an ever-increasing weight of rotundity until one reached his deep chest, broad shoulders and massive head. To me, in the first moment of excitement at meeting this renowned figure, his was the noble forehead, the smooth cap of hair, the small, penetrating eyes, straight nose, flushed cheek, square jaw and jowl of a Roman emperor.'

Maurice went on to become Warden of Wadham and Vice-Chancellor of the university, and to receive a knighthood. He was also awarded the CH, though his followers insisted it should have been the OM. When he was defeated for the Regius Professorship of Greek the outcry was almost hysterical. One eminent classical scholar announced that he would not dine in hall when the new professor came to dine there.

Maurice's greatest influence was probably exerted in the twenties and thirties. He kept his dinner guests at Wadham spellbound with a flow of witticisms that we used to compare to those of Oscar Wilde. Their flavour cannot be reproduced now; besides, some of them were on the bawdy side. When asked whether a certain head of a women's college (female, I need hardly say, in those days) was a woman dressed up as a man or a man dressed up as a woman, Maurice flashed out, 'A man dressed up as a man, of course.' A better example, perhaps, would be his definition of Oxford as 'a pause between one kind of life and another'. For years after they had gone down it was possible to distinguish Maurice's influence on some of the most gifted undergraduates.

Maurice has frequently been described as having had homosexual leanings, which may well have been true. He did, however, propose marriage to Elizabeth while she was an undergraduate and two other ladies subsequently. It may well be that my own relationship with him was affected thereby. Mary Craig, who is justly renowned for her books on the Pope, Tibet, and her deeply spiritual *Blessings*, and who honoured me by writing a biography of me which did me much more than justice, has written of me that 'men like Bowra thought he was over-rated and they refused to grant him the status of intellectual'. Nevertheless, Maurice Bowra showed more than once a friendly interest in me. He was an external examiner for the Newcastle scholarship at Eton when I was a candidate, and I was one of the two boys asked to dinner to meet the examiners. I never quite knew why, as I was certainly not in the running for the scholarship. When I became company commander of the South Ward Home Guard in 1940 he was apparently happy to serve as my second-in-command. He had a legendary First War record, though he had been hardly more than a boy at the time. He was supposed to have shot his colonel for cowardice.

I admit that Maurice did not come out to support me as Labour candidate in 1945, although he was happy to perform that task for Elizabeth in 1950. But when he was Vice-Chancellor and I was a young minister he invited me to address a gathering organised by the university and referred to me as a 'real lover of Oxford'.

Evelyn Waugh, in one of his caustic letters (in which I do not appear to much advantage myself), wrote that the young

referred to him at the end of his life as Old Tragic. No undergraduate whom I ever met or heard of would have been
impolite to Maurice in his heyday.

Elizabeth and I attracted a real collection of stars to Pakenham
Hall between 1930 and 1932, among them Evelyn Waugh,
David Cecil, John Betjeman and Anthony Powell whose marriage to my sister Violet has brought creative happiness to
both of them. My brother Edward, sister-in-law Christine, and
the background of a genuine Irish castle provided the perfect
atmosphere of literary eccentricity. David Cecil, originally a
history don and later Professor of English Literature at
Oxford, was the conversational antithesis to Maurice. Where
Maurice was a superb monologuist, David was supreme at
bringing the best out of all the company. Mary Craig quotes
him as saying something of the same kind about me, but my
skill in that direction was nothing to his. I still think that I did
John Betjeman a good turn in introducing him to his future
wife Penelope, the wonderfully original sister of my great Eton
friend Roger Chetwode. There came a time when Penelope
became a Roman Catholic, which distressed John, who was a
staunch Anglican, and may have influenced his feelings
towards me. None of my friends struck up so permanent a
relationship as he did with Edward and Christine, a friendship facilitated by his war service as British press attaché in
Dublin. On one occasion it fell to his lot to take Professor
C.E.M. Joad, then at the end of his fame, to Maynooth. Joad
for once was intimidated. He clutched John's hand nervously.
'This is formidable,' John remembered him saying.

Betjeman was regarded in those days as even more eccentric
than the rest of us. No one, I imagine, thought of him as a
future Poet Laureate. But Elizabeth, on one occasion, named
him as having had a profound influence on her by teaching
her that you could laugh at, and at the same time be totally
serious about, the same thing; for example, the Church of
England.

It was different with Evelyn Waugh and Anthony Powell. By
the time they were in their middle twenties we accepted their
status as outstanding writers with unlimited potential. Not long

ago I was asked whether I would appear in a television programme as the original Widmerpool, the comic figure who
played so large a part in *A Dance to the Music of Time*. I sought
Tony's approval. He made no objection, though assuring me
that I was not in fact the original. I must take his word for it.
But the clumsy, bespectacled Widmerpool seemed to me to
become more and more like myself as the twelve volumes proceeded. By the end he is a Labour peer who resigns from the
government, takes up youth work and dies while out for a run
with young people.

Memories of Elizabeth's friendship with Maurice Bowra have
diverted me. To recap, after my first inspiring vision of
Elizabeth just as I was leaving Oxford, I went down to seek, and
fail to find, my fortune, while she stayed at the university and
became a star. Three years later, in the summer of 1930,
prompted by a peremptory dream, I descended on
Chadlington Road and persuaded Elizabeth to join a house
party at my brother's house in Ireland.

I also, and this was more immediately relevant, obtained for
her a tutorship at a WEA summer school at Oxford. This led to
her employment as a tutor in Stoke-on-Trent, which I was still
visiting once a week. We returned to London together every
Friday night on the 1.45 AM train.

In her own book, *The Pebbled Shore*, Elizabeth has described
the steps which led her towards a lifetime's commitment to the
Labour Party. She does not usually lay much emphasis on the
radical tradition of her mother's family, the Chamberlains, or
the glamour of her great-uncle Joe. She herself refers to
Bernard Shaw as the first intellectual influence moving her to
the Left. It is a historical fact that her first encounter with the
working-class movement at the Balliol summer school of 1930
produced almost instantaneously a lifetime's decision to join
and serve the Party of the workers. Personally, I feel that her
strong religious upbringing in the Unitarian faith prepared
the way. Her father, an eminent Harley Street eye surgeon,
was a Unitarian lay minister. Her mother, like my mother,
taught her to say her prayers from the earliest days.

I would say, looking back, that my Conservatism was doomed from the moment I became engaged to Elizabeth. It was a fragile plant in any case. I remember representing the Party at some conference about that time and being described by the chairman as a 'dud' Conservative! Nevertheless, the idea of being Labour or Socialist seemed then and for some years inconceivable.

My first class in Longton was one of the original classes initiated by the great Christian Socialist, R.H. Tawney. We studied political theory and related matters. I say 'we' advisedly. The students were firmly of the belief that they had at least as much to teach us tutors, as the tutors had to teach them. My classes, which contained students of both sexes and all ages, were composed of people who, in these latter days, would probably have made their way to a university. One or two of my students did, quite late in life. The classes were non-vocational. Elizabeth, who taught English literature, and I – like other tutors – insisted on regular production of essays, but there were no examinations. While I was writing these lines, the House of Lords, on the initiative of Nora, Baroness David, a formidable expert on educational matters generally, held a debate on adult education. We were agreed that non-vocational education could have a high cultural value, which deserves strong support from the State.

During the debate, I told one story which, I am bound to say, amused the House. As I have mentioned, Elizabeth and I used to return to London from Stoke-on-Trent on Friday evening. Week by week I wooed her in the waiting room of the old North Staffordshire Hotel, which was a fairly sober place in those days. One evening the hotel manager came in and approached me aggressively: 'Look here, Pakenham,' he said, 'I can't have this kind of thing going on in a respectable hotel like the North Staffordshire.' So, rather like Adam and Eve, we were shipped out into the station waiting room. There I began to put the question and was accepted on the train. We were married at St Margaret's, Westminster, on 3 November, 1931. Sixty-three years, eight children, twenty-six grandchildren and five great-grandchildren later, I remain eternally grateful to the Workers' Educational Association, and to the hotel manager.

*

I also, in those years of experiment, tried my hand, unsuccessfully, at journalism. Peter Fleming, potential editor of the *Spectator*, installed me in their Gower Street office in his absence on his 'Brazilian Adventure'. When he returned, he found that I had been disposed of and his status imperilled. My crowning failure occurred when I was asked to investigate allegations of drunkenness at Eton. I was absurdly naïve; I called on my much revered old headmaster, C.A. Alington, only to be acidly informed: 'If you wish to perpetuate absurd libels about your old school, that is where you and I, my dear Frank, part company.'

I did not fare much better at the *Daily Mail*, where I functioned for a short while as assistant leader writer. The main leader writer, called Willy Wilson, had been in office since the late 1890s. He began by informing me: 'Our policy is that the Germans are the cruellest people in the world, except the Chinese and, of course, the Irish.' The only successful short leader I wrote was concerned with women's skirts, which the woman editor wrote for me under the heading 'Hobble Hence'. I proclaimed: 'The "hobble" is here again, very short, very precise, very plain Jane!' I was congratulated on that and on nothing else and I soon disappeared into the night.

Yet good fortune was just around the corner. To my delight and amazement, I was offered a lectureship in politics at Christ Church, with every chance of its turning into a Studentship (Fellowship). So after four years of trying my luck in London, though never leaving Oxford for long, I was back in my beloved city.

8
IRELAND

I came alive as an Irish Nationalist after I was received by Mr de Valera when he had recently been elected Taoiseach (prime minister) in February 1932. I was twenty-six, and working in the Conservative Research Department. That encounter, combined with influences described elsewhere in this book, played its part in undermining my unreflective Conservatism. I have since, more than once, described President de Valera, as he became, as the greatest statesman I have ever met. His only rival in my eyes would be Clement Attlee, whom I have described as an ethical giant; but Attlee's attitude to Christianity, as readers will find out, was distinctly cryptic. De Valera, when President, used to visit the Sacrament five times a day, but he was no bigot. His chaplain once told me that de Valera would have made an excellent Protestant.

President de Valera used to reproach me in his gentle way for not speaking Irish like my brother. He, though born in America, married a teacher of Irish. After the agreement he reached with Neville Chamberlain in 1938, I joined him at supper in the Piccadilly Hotel. He watched impassively (even then his sight was failing) an American cabaret. At the end, he turned to me and said, 'The English are a wonderful people; the Americans are a wonderful people, though they do not treat their black community as they should. Nevertheless' (after a pause) 'I think that we in Ireland can help them both on the spiritual side. The language should do something.'

Many years before I met him, de Valera had been derided for saying, 'When I want to know what the people of Ireland think, I look into my own heart.' No doubt he enjoyed a profound conviction, as was brought home to me at our first meeting, that he expressed what Rousseau would have called 'the general will', that is the real underlying will of the Irish people. But then and in the forty years during which I knew him he always expressed to me an inflexible sense of universal values rather than any narrow nationalism. I never met President Wilson, but I imagine that he conveyed the same inspiration, at the time when he seemed to offer the world a new and more glorious future; the same universal message.

Through a happy accident, and the crucial intervention of my friend Eleanor Smith, I was invited to write a book on the Anglo-Irish Treaty of 1921. It was published in 1935 under the title *Peace by Ordeal* and is still treated as a standard work. I am told, not always charitably, that it is the best book I have written.

I was lucky in a way that could not be expected to occur more than once in a lifetime. I had access to sources on both the British and the Irish sides which no doubt assisted to make that book a standard text from that day to this. I owed most of all to Robert Barton, one of the Irish signatories who signed the Treaty under (to use his own words) 'the threat of immediate and terrible war'. I stayed with him on a number of occasions, as did Elizabeth, at his romantic house in the Wicklow Hills. He gave me unlimited help, including access to a complete set of Treaty documents, quite a few of which have never been published since then. H.A.L. Fisher, who had known him in earlier days, once referred to my book, which he said 'went with an admirable swing', as a 'tribute to the uneasy conscience of Barton'.

Bob Barton was first cousin to Erskine Childers, still remembered as author of *The Riddle of the Sands*, who was Secretary to the Irish delegation and was eventually executed by his former colleagues for the part he played in the anti-Treaty side in the

resulting civil war. His widow, Molly Childers, by this time
crippled but still an arresting personality, helped to bring it all
back to me most vividly. Bob Barton showed me the place
where Erskine was arrested before being taken away to his
death. The first Lord Birkenhead, Lord Chancellor and one of
the signatories of the Treaty, had died in 1930. It was his elder
daughter, Eleanor Smith, who persuaded the publisher to
undertake the book. Michael Collins, one of the Irish signatories, still occupied a glamorous position in Birkenhead family
story-telling. He too had died, but his portraits hung on their
walls.

Austen Chamberlain, number two to Lloyd George amongst
the British signatories, read me his notes about the negotia-
tions. It was typical of his generosity, because he cannot have
liked the book, to write to me at the end: 'An honest piece of
work honestly carried out'.

Hazel Lavery, the beautiful wife of the painter Sir John
Lavery, equally attractive to British leaders like Birkenhead
and Winston Churchill, and to Michael Collins on the Irish
side, and commemorated on Irish banknotes and coins, took
me down to see Lloyd George. He was far more interested in
Hazel than in the young biographer. After he had dealt with a
few of my questions in perfunctory fashion, he saw a way out.
He seized a bell hanging in the wall and pulled it violently.
Several dogs leapt on us and further research on the book
was rendered impossible.

On the other hand, Tom Jones, the secretary of the British
delegation of 1921, talked to me generously. I am not quite
sure whether he liked the role he was represented as playing;
one that smacked of Machiavelli.

The book placed the story of the Treaty in a new light.
Hitherto, the pro-Treaty argument in England and Ireland
had had a free run. Churchill, in his memorable account in
the aftermath, for example, treated de Valera with contempt.
I myself had heard of him before I met him as 'a Portuguese
Jew or worse'. I tried to represent the final decision left to the
Irish to sign or not to sign there and then, or face 'immediate
and terrible war' as one on which honest, even heroic,
Irishmen would take different sides.

In the years that have passed, it has become more evident that Lloyd George's threat on the night of December 5, 1921, 'Sign now or else', was a bluff. The extraordinary announcement of the leader of the Irish delegation, Arthur Griffith, that he could sign even if no one else did, seems harder and harder to justify but it can always be contended that Ireland got the best deal in the circumstances. I am more convinced as time has passed that, even if that is held to be true, it was a sad day for Ireland when they signed without reference back to Dublin.

As time went on, Winston Churchill, for example, totally modified his personal attitude to de Valera. He showed him respectful attention in European gatherings. A friend of mine, Churchill's private secretary, told me that Winston was quite excited when about to receive de Valera in Downing Street more than thirty years after the Treaty.

Since publication of the book, it would be difficult to claim that I had rendered notable service to Ireland or to Anglo–Irish relations. But I was received in most kindly fashion by de Valera on many occasions. My brother Edward, not for my sake but on account of his services to the Irish theatre, was made a senator by de Valera. I had the feeling that he would not last in that role for many years. He was, strictly speaking, an Independent, but the Whip of the de Valera Party undoubtedly expected some compliance. If so, he was mistaken. I seem to remember my brother saying, 'There's someone they call the Whip, but one doesn't pay any attention to him.' When the time came for reappointment as senator, my brother's name was not on the list. De Valera felt, I think, rather guilty about this. He once told me that, looking back, he would have liked to have reappointed him but 'the pressures were very heavy'.

Soon after Catherine, my daughter, was killed, I was paying a visit to the President. Rather to my surprise, he said that his wife wished to speak to me. Her son had been killed riding in Phoenix Park. She took both my hands in hers and told me that when that happened, 'I wept for many days; now I wouldn't have him back. Please tell your wife, if you think it would help her.' Elizabeth did indeed find that the message contained a consoling truth.

I was greatly honoured by being asked to share with Dr Tom O'Neill the task of writing President de Valera's biography. Tom O'Neill did far more of the work than I did, but I think that I helped to provide a measure of perspective from the British side.

I have visited Northern Ireland many times over the years and spoken on the issues involved often in the House of Lords, although perhaps unduly aware that my remarks might be counterproductive. In my book on *Forgiveness*, published in 1989, which benefited greatly from the kind hospitality of Ann McHardy, I would like to think that I brought out something of the nobility of spirit that has shone through the terrible happenings in what President de Valera used to call 'the six counties'.

I doubt if I shall ever properly understand, let alone be regarded as understanding, the attitude of Ulster Unionists. Yet they have always been friendly to me. When I was writing my book on the Treaty in the early thirties, James Craig, then Prime Minister of Northern Ireland, welcomed me cordially as the son of my father whom he had served under in the Boer War. He showed me a stick presented to him by my father and gave me a glass of whiskey with the words, 'I am sure you prefer Irish whiskey.'

Many years later the Reverend Ian Paisley gave me a small book he had written on the Epistle to the Romans. The harsh words that I would otherwise say about his policies die away on my lips.

A man, still young, who joined the IRA on the morrow of Bloody Sunday in 1972, distributed letter bombs with lamentable effects and spent fifteen years in prison, is Shane O'Docherty, now a graduate of Trinity College and the author of an arresting book. He renounced violence in prison at a time when it might have brought down on him terrifying consequences. His book should be read by anyone who wants to understand how civilised young men can take to violence on either side.

As I write these words I can't help recalling my visit to Northern Ireland in spring 1939, when I was booked to address the students of Queen's University on partition. I was banned by the authorities but quickly transported to Newry, on the border, whence I was swiftly whisked across the frontier after my address before the large numbers of armed police could detain me. One passage from that speech comes back to me, which I admit seems a bit overblown now. 'When every constitutional channel is blocked, what wonder if idealistic men grow desperate and reach the conclusion that force is the only remedy.' If I had been denounced in the newspapers for preaching violence, and had brought a libel action, I might have suffered the same fate as my friend Harold Laski, when he used the same kind of language in a British election.

I have not been without close relationships with Protestant paramilitaries. A former member of the UDA had killed four Catholics on the instructions of his superiors. I visited him in various prisons in England and was deeply impressed by his religious conversion through the ministrations of a 'house priest'. Arising out of a debate on supergrasses in the House of Lords, I spent a very instructive night in Belfast as the guest of a paramilitary activist, in the bosom of his altogether delightful family. It was a long time since I had spent a night in a working-class home. My mind went back to Fenton (Stoke-on-Trent) in 1930. Everything was warm and human and friendly, but the shadow of violence hung over us in the sense that my host still cherished the memory of Carson and the stand made in 1912. Later he was assassinated by the IRA. Later again his wife motored me over to Armagh to call on Cardinal O'Fiach. Stupidly I left her in the car while I interviewed the Cardinal. He was horrified when he realised that she had been left outside.

At a certain point in the history of New Horizon, the youth centre which I founded with others for the homeless of Soho, two of our main social workers came from Northern Ireland – Eleanor, a Protestant, and Geraldine, Catholic. They had not known each other before they came to England but they became devoted friends. When Eleanor returned to Northern Ireland to be married in a Protestant church in Lurgan, Geraldine accompanied her as her bridesmaid. I, as chairman of New Horizon, was privileged to be invited to attend. I came away with the Irish Rugby Football Union tie presented to me by the bride's father, a large Protestant farmer. In such surroundings it seems incredible that the old religious antagonisms should not only persist but erupt all too often into murder.

I still believe that the Sunningdale Agreement and the establishment of a joint Protestant and Catholic executive in 1974 nearly succeeded. Brian Faulkner and Gerry Fitt, the leaders of the Protestant and Catholic communities, had established a relationship which was shared by their colleagues. It is a matter of history now that the wonderful opportunity was sabotaged by the Ulster workers' strike, but I shall always believe that what was so nearly achieved then will come about in the not too distant future.

What influence has being Irish had on my life? I have no doubt, looking back, that my reception into the Catholic Church owed something at least to the fact that it was the religion of Ireland. In some ways I suppose I resemble Jewish friends who possess what can only be called a dual allegiance. No one would claim that being Irish is a positive asset in a search for success in Britain. I recall, however, that President de Valera told my old friend Bryan (Lord) Moyne that my Irish understanding was likely to make me one of the few British ministers who could enter into the plight of stricken Germany. I have said earlier that being Irish has made me something of an outsider, but there are so many outsiders in prominent positions in England that there should be no whingeing on that score.

I return to my love of Ireland. 'Somewhere, sometime, somehow, Ireland caught me,' to quote a British officer who returned to become an Irish senator. To make use of another quotation, this time from the greatest of American orators since Abraham Lincoln, William Jennings Bryan: 'Some will say that I have run my course; some will say that I have not fought the fight; but no one (I hope) can say I have not kept the faith.'

9
THE YEARS OF
CONVERSION I:
Becoming a Socialist

By 1932 the most important human event in my life had already occurred. I had married Elizabeth. The most important spiritual event in my life, my reception into the Catholic Church, did not occur till January, 1940. Nevertheless, between 1932 and when war broke out, my whole approach to life was changed. When I was appointed a lecturer, they were entitled to assume that I was a sound, even a zealous young Conservative.

What were the influences that moved me so drastically from Right to Left? I cannot think of anyone in my lifetime who performed a similar somersault, unless it be Tom Mosley, who moved still further to an extreme position. When I joined the Labour Party in 1936, I announced that I did so on reading the Gospels, and under the influence of my wife. It may seem inconsistent, but when I was eventually received into the Catholic Church, I was so nervous about Elizabeth's reaction that I concealed the truth from her for a time. But looking back, there does not seem to me to have been a real inconsistency.

Elizabeth brought home to me with incomparable sincerity that all human beings are of equal worth. She was not a Christian believer when we married, but she had been brought up in a devout Unitarian household. This idea about the equality and infinite worth of all human beings has been the basis of our approach since then to all social questions. But this does not quite explain my revolutionary about-face in politics. In the last chapter, I explained how, after meeting de Valera in 1932, I developed a passion for the Irish cause second only to my brother's. My Irish dedication certainly played its part in undermining my faith in Conservatism. It should be understood that, moreover, throughout these years, I was essentially a young academic. I was employed professionally to teach politics but I had originally intended, as already explained, to be an economist. I never ceased to ask myself whether the vision of a socialist society was compatible with sound economic thinking. In other words, was a much juster distribution of wealth correlated with an improvement in the national wealth production?

Gradually, I came round to the belief that the two objectives could be achieved together, but it took me four years and, it may be thought, a good deal of personal emotion, to arrive at that conclusion.

For a while, however, I retained what now seems a curious link with the Conservative Party – indeed, with its right wing; a link not unconnected with my continuing friendship with the Birkenhead family. A colleague at Christ Church, and intimate of the Birkenheads, was Frederick Lindemann, later Lord Cherwell, Churchill's scientific adviser, and much else besides. But he was not my only connection with Winston Churchill. Just about the time when I was graduating, I had come to know Randolph Churchill. Golden-haired and incredibly good-looking, an *enfant terrible* of dramatic personality, I well remember his saying to me on one occasion, 'Freddie and Basil and Quintin may have more academic qualifications – but none of them possess what I've got, an overwhelming desire to express myself. And the tragedy of it all is –' he paused dramatically, 'I've got nothing in the whole wide world to express. I'm like an explosion that goes off and leaves the house still standing.'

Many years later he rang me up at about two in the morning and asked me to figure as one of his friends in a television programme of him at his home at East Bergholt. In a bemused kind of way I expressed myself flattered and began to discuss whether it was possible. He became impatient and rang off with the words, 'You're nothing but a bloody Socialist anyway.' However, like so many others – many who loved him, many who criticised him – I remained his friend.

In 1933, Randolph descended on me and asked me to accompany him to the Oxford Union. He was seeking to expunge a motion passed the previous week that the House would not fight for King or Country. Weakly, as usual where Randolph was concerned, I went along with him. Nothing could have been more hostile than our reception. The place was packed to the ceiling, with a large crowd outside. We were hissed and booed as we went in, with some attempts to trip us up. In spite of Randolph's brilliant oratory, I realised early that escape was our only chance of survival. As we made our way out the cry went up, 'To the Cherwell with them!' But we escaped – myself rather shattered, Randolph rather exhilarated by the experience .

Two years later, in summer 1935, I was excited to be invited by Randolph to lunch with him and his father at Chartwell. The others present were a male assistant and a female secretary. When the Grand Old Man (I realise now that he was only sixty) came in from building his wall and concocting some tremendous phrases for his *Life of Marlborough*, he was at first rather grumpy, but as the wine flowed he blossomed magnificently. The problem of the hour was how to deal with Mussolini's invasion of Abyssinia. But Churchill was already concentrating on the German menace.

'Can't you,' he asked of his spellbound little audience, 'can't you see it coming again?' I rather fatuously asked him, 'What will we do if the Germans arrive here?' 'Do? Do?' His voice took on complete authority. 'We are here,' he said, looking round, 'four able-bodied men. Our weapons', he glanced at some ancient objects on the walls, 'are not the newest. But we have a Sister of Mercy', bowing to his secretary, 'to bind our wounds. We can be sure that we will give a good account of ourselves.'

Responding to the inspiration, the same that would later cause millions to lay down their lives for freedom, and not unassisted by refreshment, we felt sure that we would acquit ourselves in that fashion. When the spell wore off, I reflected that he belonged to a past age. How little did I know what the world had in store for him, or what he had in store for the world.

My next encounter with Winston was less happy. At the beginning of the war I was seconded from the army to go over to Ireland on behalf of the Ministry of Information. (My role as a double-agent was to prove no more successful than my life as a soldier.) Churchill, First Lord of the Admiralty, was lunching with Leslie Hore-Belisha in the Savoy Grill. What I was doing there, or how I could have afforded to be there, I cannot now imagine. He spotted me as he was leaving the restaurant. 'Pakenham, isn't it?' he said to me. I explained about my going to Ireland. His tone altered and became positively choleric, as something he had heard about my friendship with de Valera returned to his mind. 'You can tell your friend *de* Valera,' he told me, 'that we have treated him with unparalleled generosity, with unprecedented liberality, and what does he do? He sinks the *Courageous*.' (A British ship had recently been sunk off the coast of Ireland.) I hung my head and looked away. Later encounters with the great man were to prove happier.

It will be recalled that, in 1935, I published my book about the Anglo-Irish Treaty, *Peace by Ordeal*, which, by Conservative ideals, was a sad departure from Unionist principles. In the corridor of the House of Lords there is a picture of the debate in the House in 1893 in which the Home Rule Bill passed by the Commons was defeated by 419 to 41 in the Lords. My father and mother's father, the Earl of Jersey, were among the peers who voted against. So completely did my book depart from these traditions that I came to feel that I was no longer a suitable member of the staunchly Tory Carlton Club, then in Pall Mall, of which I had hitherto been proud to be a member. I plucked up my courage, and sought out the genial chairman, Lord Clanwilliam, as he sat with a group of cronies in the smoking room.

'Have a glass of port, my dear boy,' he said, to put me at my ease. I could only stammer out, 'I'm afraid I want to resign from the club.' 'Resign from the club? Whatever for?' He could hardly believe his ears. 'I'm afraid I've written a book,' I began.

'Written a book, my dear boy!' he broke in. 'If all the fellows in this club who had written damn silly books left, we wouldn't have any members left.'

I hid my head and crept away. But I realised in my heart that, as a member of the Carlton Club, my time was up.

In the autumn of 1935, Elizabeth stood for Cheltenham as a Labour candidate in the General Election. This time I aimed a little lower, and approached the secretary. When I explained what my wife was about to do, he had no doubt of the hopelessness of my position. He shook my hand sadly. I had of course to resign. 'But', he added, 'if ever you are abroad' (where he seemed to think I might seek refuge) 'and in trouble, the club will always be anxious to see what they can do for an old member.'

The club barber was equally helpful. I should explain that my curls were already beginning to disappear, although I was not yet thirty. 'You have been a good customer,' he said. 'You have bought many bottles of hair oil from me. I will give you a useful piece of advice – don't buy any more from anyone. Whatever you do you will be bald within three years.' That proved to be all too true as far as the crown of my head was concerned.

Elizabeth put up a valiant fight at Cheltenham, at the time the most Conservative seat in England. I, still nominally independent, supported her on the platform. A more potent ally was Dick Crossman, generally regarded as the most brilliant of the young Socialists. He had been elected to a philosophy fellowship at New College, even before taking his schools. I can still hear him addressing the middle-class citizens at Cheltenham: 'They tell me, comrades, that there is a boom on. But what does a boom mean to working chaps like you and me?' Such language, admittedly, was part of the rhetoric of the time. Elizabeth polled well at Cheltenham, but there was never the slightest chance of her being elected.

But I was also otherwise involved during the 1935 election. My friendship with Professor Lindemann, 'The Prof', was close on the tennis court and the golf course, and at Christ Church high table I continued to support his attempts to be chosen as the Conservative MP at Oxford University. When this failed I acted on a suggestion of his to persuade A. P. Herbert to stand as an Independent. Indeed, I acted as his election agent.

Alan Herbert was a charming man and won a signal victory. I fear, however, that I earned several additional years in Purgatory for helping a candidate whose main contribution was to carry a Divorce Bill which started the rot in that direction. I can only plead that I was not a Catholic and was not, at that time, interested in the issue.

I had for some time been convinced of the moral superiority of Labour Party ideals, but could not persuade myself that they would govern the country effectively. A *Times* leading article, which could have been written by one of today's foremost Thatcherites, stated the case in the starkest terms: 'Unfortunately, wealth is like heat. It is only when it is unequally distributed that it can perform what the physicists call work.'

My support for that kind of thesis had weakened. By 1936 I suppose that I looked on the Labour Party as being at least as efficient as their rivals, and on their message as far more Christian. But I still hesitated. I have little doubt that I would have joined the Labour Party fairly soon, even had a dramatic event not precipitated my decision. In summer 1936, Sir Oswald Mosley descended on Oxford with a small army of uniformed fascist stewards. They were spoiling for a fight, as were the Oxford busmen, a very left-wing element active at that time. Sir Oswald, a dominating figure in his black uniform, standing alone on the platform in the Carfax Assembly Rooms, was repeatedly interrupted by shouts of 'Red Front'. He issued a final warning: 'The next man who says Red Front goes out.' An elegant bearded figure, in fact Basil Murray, son of Gilbert Murray, Professor of Greek, rose and said in academic tones, 'Red Front'. 'Throw that man out!' ordered Sir Oswald.

In a moment, the stewards had set on Basil Murray, the busmen had set on the stewards, and total war had broken out. I plunged into the fray and emerged eventually with slight concussion and bruised kidneys. I was never quite sure afterwards whether to portray myself as having knocked out a series of fascists or as having stood a passive martyr and allowed myself to be beaten up. Be that as it may, I joined the Labour Party soon afterwards.

At some point after the war, when Sir Oswald was seeking re-election to the Westminster parliament, a picture appeared of him being literally trodden down after a public meeting. I was horrified by the spectacle. I got on to Victor Gollancz, always the champion of the oppressed, whatever their views. Victor drafted a letter to *The Times* which we both signed, protesting that we thought poorly about this maltreatment of an eminent man.

I received a letter from Lady Diana Mosley, whom I had hardly seen for thirty years, apart from her attendance at fascist meetings at Oxford. She sought, not unsuccessfully, to puncture my self-esteem. Gollancz and I had, in the course of our letter, said that we disliked everything Sir Oswald stood for. She made that seem rather a silly comment. Some time later, Elizabeth and I were invited to dinner with Diana and 'Tom' at their flat in London. I was surprised to find what a poor opinion he had of Hitler, whom he had met only twice. He seemed to regard Mussolini much more favourably.

Years later again, when I was chairman of Sidgwick & Jackson, I wrote to Diana, then living with Tom near Paris, to ask her to do a book on the Duchess of Windsor whom she had got to know intimately. With this in mind, I went to stay with them. I can only describe him in words used recently about myself, when my daughter Antonia visited an off-licence. 'We know your father well, he's a sweet old gentleman.' That is how the brilliant tyrannical demagogue of the thirties seemed to me in his latter days.

Diana's book seems to me to be quite brilliant. The two of them lunched with me one day at my favourite haunt during my publishing days, the Gay Hussar in Greek Street, Soho. Michael Foot, most gifted of left-wing champions, was at the next table. When he left, he leant across to Tom Mosley and said in friendly fashion, 'How nice to see you back in England, Sir Oswald.' Tom Mosley did not conceal his satisfaction. 'How very English,' he remarked.

A little later, Diana was compelled to go into a London hospital with a serious tumour. I visited her there. Her son Jonathan, the present Lord Moyne, nowadays making an excellent mark in the House of Lords, quoted her as saying of the visit, 'It was so sweet and faithful of Frank to come. He thinks I am Myra Hindley.'

Later again Diana and I spoke together in a debate at Trinity College, Dublin. The subject was something abstract, but Diana knew better. She began her speech in some such fashion as this: 'A few days before the outbreak of war in 1939 I was talking to Hitler. He asked me whether Britain would fight.' The audience was riveted. She ended with a brief account of the appalling conditions in prison during the war. She received a standing ovation. I got a good reception, but nothing to hers.

But to return to the Carfax assembly rooms in 1936. As I emerged, battered but elated, I was greeted by Philip Toynbee, then a scholar of Christ Church, but in spite of the disparity of years already my friend. 'Now', he exclaimed joyously, 'you are one of us!' But it was never so simple for me. Philip was the first Communist president of the Union, though later he repudiated Communism totally, and became a leading literary critic. He tried to woo me with a concept of Christian Marxism, though he never came near to succeeding. I read a lot of Marx at that time, however, as did so many of the dons in what might be called the modern faculties. I had turned down earlier a gratifying suggestion from Warden Fisher of New College that I should write a small book in the Home University Library on Karl Marx.

10
THE YEARS OF
CONVERSION II:
Politics and Religion

The reference to H.A.L. Fisher's invitation to write a book on Marx was being penned at the moment I received a letter from John Grigg, the first-class modern historian. The House of Lords has missed much through his rejection of a hereditary peerage.

John was preparing a lecture on the temporary supersession of Hal Fisher, as an historian. He wondered if I had anything helpful to say, since I had been an undergraduate at New College when Hal Fisher was Warden. Curiously enough, I had staying with me for the weekend my son Kevin, aged forty-six, who went to New College, his wife, educated in an English convent and McGill University, and my daughter Judith's son Arthur, aged twenty-six. Kevin told me that he owed his scholarship at New College to his mastery of Hal Fisher's classic *History of Europe*. Clare said that book was one of the only two major historical works available in the library of her convent; Arthur seemed to remember a German historian called Fischer, but had no recollection of the former Warden of New College. John's thesis that Fisher had been temporarily superseded seemed to be confirmed.

Fisher, who arrived as Warden soon after I reached New College, was, looking back, more interested in me than I realised at the time. My uncle Arthur Villiers told me at the time that Hal Fisher and my father had gone for walks every

74

Sunday during their last year at Winchester, but Fisher was far too shy to mention this to me. I did not go to him for regular tutorials, but on one occasion towards the end of my undergraduate period he told me he understood I was likely to get a first. My partner at that tutorial was a huge young man, to whom Fisher remarked after he had read his essay, 'The Mens must move the Moles.' As we left the study, this friend said to me in a puzzled way, 'Do you think that was meant to be a compliment?' It was in fact the kind of cryptic utterance which was characteristic of the Warden.

After I got my first, he positively encouraged me to put in for All Souls, but owing to the concussion sustained in that fateful point-to-point I did not enter for the law school that year, or the All Souls examination. In the following year, without any preparation whatever, I went and asked for a renewed nomination. He gave it to me reluctantly, warning me I was making a mistake to enter in the circumstances. He proved entirely correct. But he did not lose his interest in me.

Apart from inviting me to write on Karl Marx, when my book on the Anglo-Irish Treaty appeared, he wrote to congratulate me, as well as making his remark to someone else about the book's being a 'tribute to the uneasy conscience of Barton'. Fisher knew Barton personally. Indeed, it was alleged that he had had a mild fling with the sister of Molly Childers, wife of Erskine Childers, who was Secretary of the Irish delegation and Barton's cousin.

Hal Fisher was, on the face of it, somewhat prim and proper, though not as prim and proper as his excellent wife. It gave us all the more pleasure, therefore, to circulate stories about his goings-on in Paris. We were proud of the fact that he had been a member of Lloyd George's cabinet as Minister of Education, but used to exaggerate the number of occasions when he would drag in this achievement. According to one story, an old New College man was enjoying himself in a brothel in Paris when he heard a well-known voice saying, '*Quand j'étais au cabinet . . .*' No one quite believed this story, but we all liked to picture the scene.

During the thirties Elizabeth and I saw quite a bit of Hal and Lettice Fisher. Left to himself he might have been quite a bon viveur, but she was famously frugal. On one occasion Hilaire Belloc came to tea. Lettice hospitably asked him, 'Will you have some tea, Mr Belloc?' Belloc brushed aside the suggestion with the words, 'I will have some wine.' Fisher, rising to the occasion, demanded of the maid, 'Some wine for Mr Belloc.' No such demand had ever been made in that household before. I don't think any wine was, in fact, produced.

On another occasion, Fisher introduced Elizabeth and me to Sidney and Beatrice Webb. She was physically one of the most impressive women imaginable, and he one of the least impressive of men. Fisher opened the conversation by asking, 'What are you talking about in Paris, Mr Webb?' He began a lucid answer, but Beatrice soon took over.

By that time I was presented as a young Socialist, and was asked to stay chez Webb at Passfield Corner. All went well till the morning of my departure, when I got involved in an argument over the Boer War in which the Webbs, surprisingly, took the anti-Boer side. Mrs Webb rebuked me with the words, 'You've forgotten your facts.' Sidney obediently repeated, 'You've forgotten your facts.' But when I left he patted me consolingly on the shoulder to help me understand that there was no ill will.

No one can deny that Fisher's three-volume *History of Europe* is a majestic work, as readable as it is scholarly. The final volume appeared in 1936, when National Socialism was already casting its shadow over Europe. It is called *The Liberal Experiment.* Young Socialists like myself could not afford to disdain it, but I think we treated its message as a prelude to our own.

Asked by John Grigg, or anyone else, what influence Fisher had on me, I recall particularly my walks with him round the University Parks in the late thirties, and the glamour he added to life, as had done the first Lord Birkenhead; both responded brilliantly to the life of politics and the enormous appeal of public service.

Though I never did write about Marx, I organised a hugely attended series of lectures on him in Christ Church Hall. Isaiah, later Sir Isaiah, Berlin (who did write the book for

Fisher, quite brilliantly) was one of the speakers, but the most spectacular lecturer of all was Roy, later Sir Roy, Harrod. A top analytical economist, Roy was a nephew of the great actor Forbes Robertson. The climax of his lecture came when he turned round and shook his fist at the portrait of a former dean of Christ Church hanging on the wall behind him. 'What are you doing there, Karl Marx, you old rascal,' he cried, 'skulking behind that long beard of yours. Come out, Marx, come out!'

I never became a Marxist, but I collaborated fully with the Oxford Communists, as we all did in the local Labour Party during that time. I took the chair, for example, for Harry Pollitt, General Secretary of the Communist Party, on his return from Spain.

'Comrades,' he cried to the packed audience in the Oxford town hall, 'you may well say to me, can a few brave men make any difference? Comrades, the International Brigade made *all* the difference.' The hall rose to him – I thought the cheering would never stop.

But they cheered just as passionately the so-called Red Dean of Canterbury, Hewlett Johnson, white-haired, pink-faced, benevolent. Wages in the Soviet Union were, he assured us, going up and up, raising his hands to heaven. Prices were going 'down, down, down', dropping his hands to his knees.

Leaving the town hall that evening, lit up with enthusiasm, I passed Father Martin D'Arcy, Master of Campion Hall, a stone's throw from Christ Church. I was already in touch with him in a timid way. He gave me the kind of look that Peter must have received from his Master, after thrice denying Him. But I was still caught up in the political world.

I was elected for the Cowley and Iffley ward of Oxford with a record vote at a by-election in 1937. In the following year I fought on a joint ticket with Abe Lazarus, the Communist organiser and a splendid demagogue. I was re-elected. He was defeated, but only just.

In autumn 1938, immediately following the Munich settlement, the Conservative for Oxford City died and a by-election followed, which not long ago was reproduced on television. I look back upon it with less pleasure than on any other event in my political life. The initiative, I still think, came from the Communists, but the feeling was widely shared in Labour and Liberal circles, that a progressive front must be formed at all costs in order to defeat the Conservative candidate, the present Lord Hailsham. We wanted to send out a message to the world that Oxford repudiated the Munich settlement.

In the event, the Labour candidate, Patrick Gordon Walker, and the Liberal candidate, were induced to stand down. A.D. Lindsay, Master of Balliol, who had helped me get my first-class degree and my first job in the WEA, was chosen as the Independent Progressive candidate. However Quintin Hogg, as he then was, always a doughty and eloquent fighter, as I was to know later to my cost, was returned the winner.

Patrick had antagonised the local Labour Party by his understandable reluctance to stand down. They began to look for another candidate. With what seems to me now extraordinary insensitivity, I put my name forward, and was chosen. Luckily, Patrick and his wife, Audrey, were very forgiving people and our friendship deepened in later years.

Providence is not always unfair. When I became candidate for Oxford, I had to abandon a candidature for West Birmingham. If I had stuck to Birmingham, I would have been elected to parliament at the general election in 1945. I was well beaten at Oxford in the same year. I had banked on Cowley and Headington, the two strong Labour wards (I was councillor for Cowley) being brought into the parliamentary area. But this did not happen. Shall we say, I got my deserts. Patrick Gordon Walker was quickly elected to the House of Commons after the war and was a cabinet minister by 1950.

The Labour Club at Oxford was dominated by Communists – Denis Healey, who has done great things since, among them; Harold Wilson was, in those days, a Liberal. One of my pupils stood bravely and eloquently for Democratic Socialism – Chris Mayhew, now Lord Mayhew. When he was President of the Union, I rated high his chance of one day becoming a Labour prime minister.

Family life went forward apace. Elizabeth was at least as active in the Cowley Labour Party as I was – we attended meetings of one kind or another every night. By the time the war came, she had brought into the world three children: Antonia, Thomas and Paddy. She was Labour candidate for Kings Norton, Birmingham. As the war went on she had three more children: Judith, Rachel and Michael and resigned her candidature. As things turned out, she would have been elected by many thousands of votes. Instead, she went on to have two more children, Catherine, who was to die tragically in 1969, and Kevin. Every now and then nowadays when a politician disappears from office, we are told that he hopes to see more of his family. Ernest Bevin and Hugh Dalton once told me that Elizabeth would have had a great career in politics. No doubt that is true, and no doubt she sacrificed it for her family.

There was another side to my thoughts and feelings which became increasingly urgent as the thirties drew to an end. As I have explained, I was brought up to say my prayers by my mother, a practice I have maintained and indeed extended, as I move towards the end of my eighties. At Eton, I had come under the inspiring influence of Cyril Alington. I still think of him as the greatest preacher I have listened to and saw him quite often for private discussions. Yet, for reasons that are still not quite clear to me, I never attended college chapel at Oxford, and was at best a feeble Anglican.

Christ Church was equipped with a rich variety of illustrious theologians, canons and professors. One of them, an especially notable thinker, Professor Williams, was the father of my much-admired younger friend in the House of Lords, now Lord Williams of Elvel. In the eight years that I spent as chairman of the National Bank, and in all the years since, I have never met anyone else who could be described as a Socialist expert on the inner workings of the City. His mother rendered help of untold value to Elizabeth as she gradually moved through the Church of England to join me in the Catholic Church. And but a few yards away from Christ Church dwelt – I had almost said lurked – Father Martin D'Arcy of Campion Hall.

No one except Elizabeth, and possibly my uncle Villiers, has influenced me so much as Father D'Arcy, Chaplain of Campion Hall, did in the twenties and thirties. Later, he spent a short unhappy period as a provincial before dying in the sixties revered by all. He was a unique figure in the Oxford I knew as undergraduate and don. I would submit that no individual had so great an influence on such a wide circle of intellectuals and others. Maurice Bowra, the Oscar Wildean wit, who inspired so many with a love of knowledge for its own sake; J.C. Masterman, hockey international, high-jump Blue, first-class cricketer, who once made his way into the last eight at Wimbledon, wise counsellor to generations of athletes; G.D.H. Cole, whose Socialist circle attracted so many who achieved eminence afterwards, including Hugh Gaitskell – all these might be put forward as having made an impression on many people. But no one, I feel sure, went so deep with so many as Martin D'Arcy (though I never called him Martin in his lifetime, either to his face or even behind his back).

The cleverest undergraduates who took Greats (ancient history and philosophy) were inclined to be intellectually snobbish, if they will forgive the word. They admired sheer intellect, most of all dialectical intellect. Father D'Arcy was equal to every demand on him of that kind. Dick Crossman, Douglas Jay and, especially, Quintin Hogg made friends with him. Quintin was asked to preach at the memorial service for Father D'Arcy in Campion Hall, though he had never quite succumbed to the charms of the Catholic Church.

But Father D'Arcy was a philosopher. Reading again his book, *Christian Morals*, first published in 1937, I came across this passage: 'The degree of culture reached by any people will be measured by its moral ideals, its artistic achievements, its science and its religion.' The breadth of his own culture comes to me afresh as I recall the high regard in which he was held by my close friend at that time, 'Prof' Lindemann, later Lord Cherwell, professor of experimental philosophy, and W.H. Auden, amongst other poets.

I cannot quite remember when I first met Father D'Arcy. Elizabeth recalls meeting him in the late twenties, at a lunch given by Murrough O'Brien, a devout if ebullient Catholic. He was slim, dark in those days, aristocratic-looking – he was proud of his Norman ancestry; distinctly mysterious, and faintly sinister in Elizabeth's eyes. After lunch, however, in trying to help her on with her coat, he placed it the wrong way round, which she found reassuringly human. As she tells me this story, I must believe it, but it is very unlike my recollection of him, at ease in all situations.

While I was moving towards the Church, Elizabeth was anxious about his influence over me. Many years after she herself was received, at the time of Catherine's death, he provided her with inexpressible comfort. Evelyn Waugh was received by him in 1930. I was not received till ten years later, when Father D'Arcy had gone to America on war service. During those years, Evelyn exerted a steady pressure on me; there was therefore a curious link between him, Father D'Arcy and myself. I shall always feel honoured and proud that even before I was received into the Church Evelyn invited me to be godfather to Auberon, his newborn eldest son, now justly famous.

When, in the late 1930s, I felt that I could wait no longer to try to systematise my Christianity, I turned instinctively to Martin D'Arcy. It must not be thought that my conversion was as described in a review of a book of mine in *The Times*, as an affectionate tumble into Father D'Arcy's arms. I read more theology in the three years before the war than I have in any comparable period since. Evelyn used to say that Father D'Arcy kept his converts on the edge of the Church. If there was any truth in this, it would lie in the extraordinary joy that he himself clearly found in it. It may be I hesitated timidly to share it.

In the event, Father D'Arcy was despatched to America on war service at the outbreak. I was on leave from the army in Oxford, and woke up one morning with the overwhelming certainty that I must delay no longer. I was received into the Franciscan church, the Grey Friars, in Iffley Road, in January, 1940.

At the time I was received, Elizabeth was full of suspicion. She identified the Catholics, as did some of my left-wing friends, with reaction, and in particular with support for Franco in the Spanish Civil War. In the six years that followed she gradually made her way towards Catholicism. She was given enormous help by Muriel Williams, wife of the memorable Regius Professor and colleague of mine at Christ

Church, Nippy Williams. Muriel guided her with infinite sensitivity through the stages that led from Humanism through Anglicanism to Catholicism. Muriel and Nippy's son Charles, assisted always by his wife Jane, niece of Rab Butler and former probation officer, has played a part of the utmost distinction in the House of Lords. I would dearly like to have seen him become the Leader of the Labour peers, although our present incumbent Ivor Richard is a man of the highest quality and credentials. As our revered Chief Whip Ted Graham said to me at the time, 'Charles is a big man and he will put up with this adversity.'

Towards the end of the 1930s I was involved in the social activity for which I suppose I am best remembered today. In the *Guardian* as I write, I am described as a penal reformer; and certainly, if two words are going to be used about me after my death, I am happy that those should be the two. People often ask, how did I get involved in prison work? I suppose it all began with my desire to plumb the depths of human misery. By the late thirties, I was an Oxford city councillor with rooms in Christ Church. It was a short step to the Oxford prison where I became a so-called official visitor.

My first prisoner was a respectable solicitor who was at pains to explain to me how appalling it was for him to find himself in this situation. I believed every word he said, but learnt a lesson quickly afterwards. It was explained to me that he had been in prison many times for one of kind of fraud or another; this time, for marking eggs incorrectly or not marking them at all – I cannot remember which. There was an absurd rule at the time that prison visitors were not supposed to keep contact with their prisoners when the latter were released. Somewhat later, my admired friend Victor Gollancz refused to sign a pledge to this effect, and was therefore blackballed as a potential prison visitor. I compromised by offering the prisoners breakfast at our home in North Oxford, sometimes with a glass of wine. Elizabeth joined in my welcome, and from that day to this has supported my every move on behalf of prisoners.

11
UNDERGRADUATE FRIENDS

I like to think that I was quite a successful tutor. I could not equal the record of Oliver Franks, later ambassador in Washington, head of two Oxford colleges, a peer, and all sorts of things; it was said that all his pupils got firsts, which is not credible, but he was undoubtedly quite exceptionally successful in that direction. I can't remember that anyone got a first when I was teaching, but then no one was expected to in Modern Greats in Christ Church. When I reappeared in the fifties, it was quite different; I will mention only Nigel Lawson and Roger Opie. I thoroughly enjoyed teaching and can honestly say that I was dedicated for seven years to my pupils. I doubt if I could have kept it up much longer.

I did nothing much on the lecturing circuit – oddly, because I was making a good many political speeches by the time the war came. I think that I lacked the dogmatism and the scholarship which make the great lecturer, like Alan (A.J.P.) Taylor.

I played games with any of my pupils who were that way inclined, and like to think that I was on good terms with all or most of them. I would only mention three, however, who I could say became real friends – Philip Toynbee, Chris (now Lord) Mayhew and Nico (now Lord) Henderson, who all came from what may be called establishment backgrounds. Philip's father, Arnold Toynbee, was at that time a world-famous historian; his mother Rosalind, a Catholic convert, wrote a

memorable book called *The Good Pagan's Failure*. His grandfather was Professor Gilbert Murray, his grandmother Lady
Mary Murray, both resident at Boar's Hill and present to the
consciousness of Oxford. Gilbert Murray had started life as a
Catholic. On his deathbed it was said by his daughter Rosalind
that he returned to the Church. In the meanwhile, he was a
leading, perhaps the leading, academic agnostic. Lady Mary
was connected with every sort of aristocratic family; her
mother was famous for pouring away the family supply of
priceless wines. She and Gilbert were fanatical teetotallers and
vegetarians. I only learned recently that Gilbert had been an
alcoholic in early days.

Chris Mayhew's father, though less glamorous, was distinguished in his own world of chartered accountancy, and was
well understood to be a wealthy man. Nico's father was, by the
time of the war, Warden of All Souls, having previously been
closely associated with Maynard Keynes as a Cambridge economist. His book, *Supply and Demand,* was in my time more read
than any other economics textbook. His mother came from
the very heart of Bloomsbury. Nico had been educated in
those circles before he went to Stowe.

All three were athletic; Chris, notably so. I can still see Philip
Toynbee playing wing forward for Christ Church when they
won the college rugby football championships. I can still hear
his more eminent blind-side colleague, Chris Mayhew's
brother, an Oxford Blue, giving him the final instruction:
'Wing like Hell, Toyners!' Chris was decidedly a most distinguished man. Coming from Haileybury, where he had been
sportingly pre-eminent, he could, I am assured, have won
Blues for rugger, cricket and long jump. Instead he devoted
himself to politics and good causes. Nico, though afflicted at
one time by polio, was still playing good tennis at the age of
seventy.

All three were idealistic. Philip was the first Communist president of the Oxford Union. There was a moment when he saw
his way to recruit me, but I suppose that my Christianity prevented me from going over the brink. He had been expelled
from Rugby for his adventures in student journalism, but
gained a scholarship to Christ Church after studying at

Ampleforth. After he went down and I came into an unexpected legacy, I appointed him editor of the Birmingham
Labour Party paper, the *Town Crier*, on which I expended a
good deal of the legacy. At the time of Munich, he and I
fought shoulder-to-shoulder in Edgbaston, of all extreme
Conservative places, and announced we would make
Edgbaston too hot for Neville Chamberlain. In later years,
Philip became a very eclectic form of Christian and found
much happiness with his second wife Sally.

Chris was the only prominent Labour undergraduate who
was not a crypto-Communist. He risked death many times during the war. He was greatly valued by Attlee, not only because
he was an old Haileyburian. For one reason or another he
found his way to the Liberal Party, always maintaining a strong
interest in those who needed his help, from the mentally disturbed to the Arabs.

Nico has now been my friend for well over fifty years and I
was so pleased he undertook the task of proposing the health
of Elizabeth and me when Antonia gave a party for us on the
occasion of our sixtieth wedding anniversary. He has won enormous fame as ambassador in Poland, Germany, France and
the United States. Few would dispute my submission that he is
the best-looking of ambassadors in recent years. Tall, with thick
grey hair and a strong, humorous expression, he is just what
the public imagine an ambassador ought to look like. When I
first knew him he was a supporter of the Labour Party. Many
years later he seemed to have moved to the right, but at all
times he has been a British patriot, increasingly convinced in
recent years that the future of Britain lies with Europe.

All were highly articulate; all were Presidents of the Union;
I do not wish to give the impression that I only selected friends
who were Presidents of the Union, it just happens that all
three were. In later years, Philip became a leading book
reviewer, writing a weekly column for the *Observer*. Chris at a
certain point was a television star. Nico has written two brilliant
books, the second a triumph in the face of strenuous
opposition.

Philip's religious books, highly original, would need to be
quoted at length if at all. I will select instead the final passage

of his book *Friends Apart*, a memorial of his two friends killed in their youth, one in the British army, one fighting on the Republican side in Spain. Both came from distinguished backgrounds. Jasper Ridley married the daughter of Violet Bonham Carter, and was a social star at Oxford. Esmond Romilly, a nephew of Winston Churchill, ran away from Wellington to start a revolutionary paper. Philip got himself expelled from Rugby in the course of assisting him. But this is how he finished the joint tribute:

> Yet my two friends had, I think, more authority and more freedom than most people have. Each showed himself capable of change; one did what he wished to do and the other thought as he wished to think; both were positive young men with sharp and effective personalities. Most of us are more tightly held down than either of them was, and I have written this book as a tribute to freedom – in action, in thought and in feeling – as well as to show again how outer and inner circumstances compel us along our own paths.

I have had many happy times with all three, Chris, Philip and Nico. I remember staying in a hotel at Rugby with Philip, near his old school. I think we were on our way to support Philip Noel-Baker in a by-election; at any rate, it was when the Emperor of Abyssinia was in England. I introduced Philip to a waiter as the Crown Prince of Abyssinia. He was admittedly a little bit swarthy. The waiter said, 'God bless you, sir, and may God bring you back to your own.' I hope we both felt thoroughly ashamed over the deception.

Chris has joined me in recent years in the House of Lords, where I always boast of him as my old pupil. When he was a young man I forecast he could be prime minister. That is not likely now, but when I hear him speak today, I don't find it difficult to remember why I made the forecast.

At various times, I lived in Nico's house in Charlotte Street, in Sussex Gardens and in his present home in Fairholt Street. Elizabeth and I have also been his guests in Paris, Vienna and Washington. I remember making my way back from Vienna without my passport which I had somehow mislaid, passing many frontiers, heaven knows how. We visited Washington for the wedding of my son Michael, Nico's godson, to the very talented Mimi. Nico has sometimes remarked that I was best man at his wedding; I would have liked to have been, but Louis MacNeice was selected.

It is quite lamentable in my eyes that Nico, the most distinguished diplomat of his time, was never made a member of the House of Lords. One might say the same of Michael Palliser, head of the foreign service. Margaret Thatcher has many virtues but her strange antipathy to the foreign service must be placed on the other side of the ledger. Nico and I have had much fun together. When we visited the chess championships in Hastings, a board was abandoned at a certain point and we took over. A crowd gathered round us, watching every move with fascinated expectancy. When I was forced to put the question of how one castled, a look of horror passed across their faces, and they disappeared at once.

Nico has been a wonderful godfather to Michael, who was formerly ambassador in Luxemburg. I am torn between a desire to attribute his success to Nico's support and a refusal to admit that any kind of nepotism has helped him along. At any rate, he has been very successful and I shall always think that the choice of Nico as his godfather was inspired.

The Private Office, Nico's account of life with five foreign secretaries, is full of vivid recollections. He portrays Anthony Eden as having had a tremendous interest in military matters (though he does not refer to Eden's glorious record in the First War as a very young man). Nico also describes him as a great reader of the classics – French, English and Persian. In the early twenties, before Eden went into politics, he wrote a paper about the French Impressionists. Nico is content to describe him as 'an aesthete', who could bring to politics the qualities of an artist. One of Eden's outstanding qualities, according to Nico, was confidence, not only in himself but also in those who worked most closely with him.

Rab Butler is presented as incurably indiscreet, which Nico curiously seems to feel worked out to his advantage. After Rab had left politics, Nico ran into him in the foyer of the Festival Hall. The news of Alec Home's resignation as the Leader of the Tory Party had just been announced. "It's so sad, isn't it?" he said to me. "I mean, Molly says it shows I made a great mistake [letting slip the chance to succeed Home] but you don't think so, do you? I say it's very sad; I mean, for Alec.'"

In his book, Nico restricts his imagination, but every now and then he indulges his fancy. When Labour won the election in 1964, Butler had to make way for Gordon Walker. 'Rab was determined to make the best dramatic use of the occasion. Realising that, after some forty years in public life, he would never hold office again, he clearly did not intend to skimp his farewell performance. He told us how happy our prospects were compared with his. He would miss it all very much. It would never be the same again. Renouncing the use of an official car and stepping out from the side door of the Foreign Office into the Horse Guards, his withered arm at his side, he set off across the park glancing up at the sky as if he saw in its newfound limitlessness something as full of foreboding as did Oscar Wilde's condemned murderer in looking up at the little tent of blue. He was a free man, yet after all those years he dreaded being without the bonds of office.'

On the day Winston Churchill retired from office in 1955, Rab sent him the following lines by St Augustine:

> *Let nothing disturb me*
> *Let nothing afright thee*
> *All passeth away*
> *God alone will stay*
> *Patience obtaineth in all things*

Was he muttering these words to himself as he left office for the last time?

Me aged nine

Aged three (*second from left*) with Pansy, Edward and Mary,
1909

Elizabeth, 1931

Me in 1931

Our wedding, St Margaret's, Westminster, 1931

Judith's christening

In the ranks of the
Oxford & Bucks, T.A., 1939

With Thomas, Paddy and Antonia, 1938

Race round Christ Church meadows, 1935

As Minister of Civil Aviation, 1948-51

The Pakenham children at 10 Linnell Drive, 1950:
(*from left*) Judith, Antonia, Catherine, Rachel, Kevin,
Paddy, Michael and Thomas
(*back row, kneeling*) Paddy, Thomas, Judith; (*front row*) Catherine,
Antonia, Kevin, Rachel, Michael

Elizabeth and me as Victoria and Albert at Catherine's
21st birthday party,
1967

Giving Rachel away, 1967

With Richard Nixon and Charles Forte

With Harold Pinter and Cricketers

Our Golden Wedding, 1981 (*Lord Lichfield*)

Flora and Stella,
Blanche and Rebecca,
me, Antonia, Elizabeth,
1992

With Elizabeth, Antonia, Stella and Flora, 1993. (*Lord Lichfield*)

With my great-granddaughter Stella. (*Lord Lichfield for* Hello)

12
THE WAR
1939–45

I have tried so far to avoid my previous writings, but I cannot improve on what I wrote forty years ago about my role in the war:

> Millions of men, women and children are estimated to have been killed in the war. Millions more were permanently disabled. No one can measure the number of ruined lives. Many men and women performed feats of undying heroism. Many more proved themselves quietly equal to every effort and sacrifice required of them. Some there were who did their best, but who proved sadly unable to play the part that they and perhaps others had expected. In this category I must take my place.

My family were above all things military: soldiers, generals sometimes, the occasional admiral. My great-great-uncle, Wellington's brother-in-law, was killed leading British troops at New Orleans against the Americans. My father was killed leading his brigade at Gallipoli. His last recorded words, according to his ADC, later Colonel Cripps, brother of Stafford Cripps, were in character: 'What are you ducking for, Fred? The men don't like it. And it doesn't do any good.'

In spring 1939 I joined the Territorials as a private. It was considered, in Oxford, a peculiar step. I was a thirty-three-year-old don, recently chosen as the Labour candidate for the City and well known as an active campaigner for Socialism in conjunction with the Communists. The *Oxford Mail* showed me offering a cigarette to a fellow private with the words, 'Have a fag, mate.' In other words, I was portrayed as attempting a contradictory and even ludicrous role. As recently as 1935, it had been possible for Sir Stafford Cripps to cry, at a Labour conference, 'I will never ask the workers of this country to place themselves under the military machine.' In other words the Labour Party, though not pacifist, were at heart antimilitarist. Clem Attlee, Major Attlee as he was still referred to, had a most glorious war record, having seen, as Churchill generously said of him, the hardest fighting on many fronts, but so unobtrusively that he was never mentioned in despatches. But Attlee, whatever he may have felt in his heart, led the Labour Party in 1939 in opposing conscription.

My joining the Labour Party was a feeble kind of attempt to be a good Socialist and at the same time my father's son. I ought to explain that my uncle Arthur Villiers, who inspired my whole approach to social work, had served in the trenches throughout the First War. He could never quite think the same of any officer who had left the trenches to serve on the staff. For me also, therefore, service must be service in the front line. When I went to Territorial camp in 1939, I was, I must admit, horrified by the language which persisted in our tent through the night. 'Effing' is so much commoner today than it was then; perhaps I would not now receive such a cultural shock. At the time, however, I was quite overwhelmed and undeniably influenced. When I went home on leave, I shocked the vicar by my language on the tennis court.

I survived Territorial camp, and when war broke out I was gazetted as a second lieutenant. I can't pretend that I was much more at home with my young officer colleagues, Conservative to a fault. It is not unfair to recollect one conversation which took place when I was detached from my regiment and attached to a mixed group of officers guarding the Isle of Wight.

Senior Captain at breakfast to me, the newcomer: 'You may care to know what papers we take – *Telegraph* for the news,

Express for the headlines, *Mirror* for the cartoon. No further suggestions, I suppose?'

I, loyally and rather defiantly: 'Yes, I would like to suggest that we take the *Daily Herald.*'

Gasps of genuine astonishment and horror.

Senior Captain: 'What a paper to take in an officers' mess!'

I: 'The *Herald* suits me because I happen to be a Socialist.'

Senior Captain, authoritatively: 'All Socialist politicians are bloody fools.'

Friendly, slightly sycophantic Subaltern, trying to act as peacemaker: 'Can't we agree that all politicians are bloody fools, otherwise we shouldn't be in this bloody awful place?'

Grunts and titters all round. I don't suppose that episode would have been so likely to occur in the later stages of the war.

But for every absurdity I could discover in my fellow officers they could discover a hundred in me. They also were having to make adjustments, perhaps at least as painful as mine, and they succeeded in making them and I didn't.

I began to suffer from recurrent doses of influenza. I went into a lonely church on the Isle of Wight and prayed that my cup might pass away from me:

> *And as I prayed it seemed to matter less*
> *To win a miracle to set me free.*
> *Somewhere the hand of God stretched out to bless;*
> *My prayer was answered though not answered me.*

But the doses of influenza continued. I was given a week's leave. I spent a month in a nursing home. Nancy Astor visited me and read St John's Gospel to me. I didn't dare tell her that I had become a Roman Catholic. Douglas Woodruff also came, playing chess as competitively as ever and beating me even more easily than usual. I appeared before a Medical Board and, admittedly to my enormous relief, was told that I was being invalided out. Elizabeth stood by me heroically as anyone who knows her would expect. Here, however, beyond question, was failure: complete and absolute failure.

I would not wish that kind of failure on anyone, but it has

had compensations. In later years, when I have visited prisoners sometimes despised by the world and suffering total disgrace, I have been able to say, or at least convey the thought, that I also have been humiliated.

Not so long ago, when I was about to open a debate in the House of Lords, I visited a prison where a number of sex offenders were held and spent an afternoon in discussion with them. I shook hands with the group when I left, but when I came to the last one, formerly a highly respected headmaster, I became overwhelmed by a sense of the humiliation that he must be feeling. Words came to me, I cannot say from where. I said to him, 'We're both sinners'; but I used a rougher word than sinners. The words came from my heart and I think went straight to his.

I was treated with extreme consideration by the military authorities. In a worldly sense, it was almost a miracle for me, certainly a merciful stroke of providence, that the Home Guard was formed when I returned for a time to teach at Christ Church. I became a major in the Home Guard, flaunting a crown on my shoulder. I worked frantically as a company commander, to atone for my failure in the real army. We were unbelievably belligerent – almost literally praying that the enemy would arrive in Oxford so we could give him a bloody nose. We had, if I remember rightly, five rounds apiece for our Canadian rifles.

Unlike many whose records were altogether more glorious, I sustained a wound on pseudo-active service. One night there was a warning that the Germans were on their way – false as it turned out. We sprang to arms on the Abingdon Road. Eventually the order to unload was given. The Christ Church College cook, instructed by me in musketry, did not perform the operation successfully. He fired the last bullet into the ground and it ricocheted into one of my feet which still bears the more or less honourable marks of my war service.

I was removed to the Radcliffe Hospital. The foot was sewn up, but in such a way that the splinters remained within. The doctor, encouraging me, drew a line round my ankle, explaining that if they had to operate, it would not be any further up.

In the end, it all passed off happily, with my signing a statement for pension purposes that the wound was not self-inflicted.

In 1941 another stroke of luck arrived at a time when I was much in need of it. Sir William (Lord) Beveridge asked me to act as his personal assistant. I served in that capacity for three years, during which he carried out four inquiries. He investigated the use of skilled manpower in the services, fuel rationing, what would now be called social security, and full employment. It was the third of these which made him a world-famous figure.

On the morning the report came out, I went into my local newsagent and asked for a morning paper, to be told they were sold out. 'It's that Sir William Beveridge,' explained the shopkeeper. 'He's going to abolish want.' And fifty years later no one can deny that he made an enormous contribution to that end.

I would select four outstanding qualities possessed by Beveridge: one, intense humanitarian zeal; two, first-class knowledge of the social services; three, sheer brain power; four, self-assurance. The first two qualities have been possessed by not a few others I have known or worked with, but in his combination of the last two qualities Beveridge was unique in my experience. Champions of J.M. Keynes and Bertrand Russell must make claim on behalf of their heroes, but neither possessed the understanding of administration which was an additional element in Beveridge's case.

Few, if any, surpassed his academic record; he took first-class honours in Maths, Classical Moderations and Greats at Oxford and was for many years director of the London School of Economics. His self-assurance I will illustrate with one anecdote. When he had completed his report on the use of skilled manpower in the services, he was invited to the War Office to be received by the Secretary of State for War. I, as usual, tagged along behind him, metaphorically carrying his bag. We were ushered into the Secretary of State's room. Beveridge sat on one side of the table, a civilian member of his committee on each side of him; I perched nervously behind him. Opposite us the Secretary of State, later Lord Margesson, was surrounded by top brass covered in medals.

David Margesson leaned forward impressively. 'I'm sure, Sir William,' he said, 'that you will agree that our arrangements are very satisfactory.' Beveridge paused – my son-in-law, Harold Pinter, would have recognised him as a master of the pause. Then he delivered his verdict. 'A miserable show,' he said. He paused again. He was not sure that he had made a sufficient impact. 'A mis-er-able show.' This time there was no doubt of the impact, which left the Secretary of State and the assembled top brass in a state of total confusion.

Nearly all doors were open to Beveridge. He was welcomed at Buckingham Palace and almost – but not quite – everywhere else. Churchill, when still a member of the Liberal cabinet, had helped advance Beveridge's career. When the great man became Prime Minister, Beveridge wrote to him suggesting an interview. Churchill wrote back grandiosely and snubbingly. As I recollect the letter, not perhaps quite accurately, it ran: 'Nothing would give me greater pleasure, my dear Beveridge, than to receive one who rendered me such useful services in earlier days. But some of us, alas, are burdened with the task of winning the war and so our encounter will have to wait until happier days.'

Apart from Churchill, one other person who did not join in the general adulation of Beveridge at that time was Evelyn Waugh. Now that I was a Catholic, as well as Auberon's godfather, I felt close to Evelyn. One day during the war I had arranged to give him lunch at the Savoy. How could I ever have afforded it? As I was leaving the office I ran into Beveridge and asked him to join us. The conversation between Beveridge and Evelyn went badly from the beginning, and finished this way:

Waugh: 'How do you get your main pleasure in life, Sir William?'

Beveridge: 'By trying to leave the world a better place than I found it.'

Waugh: 'I get mine from spreading alarm and despondency, and I am sure that I get more pleasure than you do.'

Beveridge was not easily ruffled but that afternoon he kept

repeating to me, 'He is a crack-brained fellow, isn't he?'

Beveridge had a form of academic humour that left me sometimes wondering whether or not he was intending to amuse. When I was working with him on social security, he was asked by the government to undertake as a sideline an inquiry into fuel rationing. In the course of our investigations, we repaired to Edinburgh where Beveridge addressed a large gathering of fuel overseers. He had beside him Mrs Mair, as she then was, his long-time companion, whom he married when her husband died and who was incidentally always very favourable towards me.

Beveridge began the meeting in this way: 'I rise to greet you, and if you will allow me I will now continue sitting. I have at my side Mrs Mair who was associated with me in bacon rationing in the First War.'

The Scottish fuel overseers sniggered into their notebooks. Sitting behind Beveridge's chair I was not quite sure where to look.

People have often asked me whether Beveridge was a Labour sympathiser. To that there is no easy answer. He had been a Liberal previously, I suppose, and he became a Liberal candidate, indeed a Liberal, in 1944. But there was a moment when he could have joined the Labour Party, and in that case he would have certainly been a leading member of the post-war Labour cabinet.

Arthur Jenkins, father of Roy Jenkins, a widely respected Labour MP and PPS to Attlee, Deputy Prime Minister, per-suaded Attlee to give a little dinner party for Beveridge at the Oxford and Cambridge Club. We sat down to dinner; Attlee, Beveridge, Arthur Jenkins and I. Unfortunately, nothing could have gone worse. After dinner, first Attlee fell asleep and then Beveridge – or was it the other way round? Eventually Jenkins and I aroused them and a little procession moved along Pall Mall: Attlee and Beveridge in front, we acolytes behind. Arthur Jenkins, sweetest of men, turned to me and said, 'I think it went pretty well, don't you?' As I explained, nothing could have gone worse.

Shortly after, Beveridge officially joined the Liberal Party. The Beveridge Report and Beveridge himself are now part of history; it was a tremendous privilege for me to have served him for three years. If people ask whether I had a good war, I have to say that it was very inglorious, but, in the event, quite useful.

I am rather inclined to boast about having known Evelyn Waugh, as well as George Orwell and Graham Greene – the writers of my generation, though a little older than I.

Stories such as the one I have just told about Evelyn and Beveridge are somewhat plentiful, and don't give a fair impression of my friend. He has been called a snob, but someone else who was called a snob – John Buchan, infinitely kind to me when I was an undergraduate – said to me: 'When you reach my age, you will realise that what people call snobbery is a longing for romance.' Evelyn was a romantic through and through. He was the bravest of the brave in the war, until sidelined by his superiors as being rather too much of a handful for regimental life.

Randolph Churchill used to tell a wonderful story – which could only have come from Evelyn – of Mountbatten, Head of Combined Operations, receiving Evelyn, who was being returned to his unit from the Commandos. The story begins with Mountbatten welcoming Evelyn effusively: 'Ah, my dear Evelyn, it is a great pleasure to meet you; I have enjoyed your books so much. Sit down, my dear fellow, have a whisky and soda, and a cigar.'

Evelyn begins to melt visibly. Mountbatten continues: 'I have not been worried so much for a long time as I have been about the trouble you are having with Charles Hayden [the Brigadier responsible for Evelyn's transfer]. I would have gone into it myself, but Winston insists I go with him to Quebec – and you know what Winston is!'

What follows must be Randolph's fabrication. 'Charles is a good fellow – but he has not been brought up like you and I have.' (Charles was some kind of Scottish laird, Evelyn the son of a publisher.) '*Noblesse oblige*, you know what that means, Evelyn. Don't you think the big thing is to laugh at old Charles?' Evelyn, in the story, surrenders completely and agrees not to press his complaint. Mountbatten's attitude

96

changes instantaneously. He presses a bell; a secretary prances in on high heels, with a form beginning: 'I, Captain Waugh, renounce all claims . . .' Evelyn signs bemusedly. Mountbatten returns to his papers dismissively.

I put this story once to Evelyn, who agreed with it in substance though dissenting in detail; but the Randolph version was the one we all used to enjoy. No one, in the light of it, could say that Evelyn did not have a good sense of humour about himself.

Evelyn was a very affectionate man. I first came to know him because my sister Pansy shared a house with his first wife in Islington, before she married him. I attended his wedding breakfast and used to make a pilgrimage to see him every year. Even before *Decline and Fall* came out, he was spoken about as a great writer in the making. After his divorce, he and I, based on the Savile Club, hunted in couples and might be said to have climbed the social ladder together, although I did not come to know his close aristocratic friends, the Lygons of later *Brideshead* fame, the Brownlows or, at that time, Diana Cooper. He was an immensely acceptable guest at Pakenham Hall, where he, with John Betjeman, Maurice Bowra and David Cecil, somehow mated the best of Oxford with the best of Irish culture.

He was very severe on the manuscript of an autobiographic work of mine called *Born to Believe* (1952), but appeased me by pointing out that there had been no good prose writing in England since 1900. His own prose idols were Swift, Matthew Arnold and Newman. Hazlitt he rated slightly lower. I learned from his published diaries that, leaving Pakenham Hall in August 1930, he was received into the Catholic Church a month later by Father Martin D'Arcy. In a sense he compartmentalised his life. I had not had the faintest idea that this step was in his mind.

Brideshead Revisited, when it came out in 1943, rather depressed me. There were aspects of his Catholicism which put me off, but not seriously. I respected him to the end of his life as a first-class Catholic of a very conservative temper. The best account known to me of Evelyn as a human being was written by my friend Richard Acton, a rising star in the House of Lords, when he is able to attend. Under the heading: '*Will a lion come?*' – *Memories of Evelyn Waugh,* Richard's article appeared in the *Spectator* of 19 September 1992. I will quote one passage here: 'Evelyn Waugh died on Easter Sunday 1966 at the age of sixty-two. To the world at large he was a ferocious literary lion. We were lucky; to our family he was much more than that. He was warm and generous and stimulating and funny. When I think of Evelyn Waugh, I remember how I held him in awe when he roared, but above all I remember his infectious laugh.'

13
AFTER THE WAR
1945–48

Sherlock Holmes's Dr Watson said, if I remember rightly, that 'the Afghan war brought honour and glory to many, but to me, nothing but a serious wound.' I suppose the same could be said of my war experiences.

It could also be said of what happened to me in the post-war general election. I was comfortably beaten at Oxford by Quintin Hogg (later Lord Hailsham), the sitting member, at a time when my Socialist contemporaries such as Hugh Gaitskell, Dick Crossman, Evan Durbin, and soon afterwards Patrick Gordon Walker, were triumphantly returned to the Commons.

I have always thought that I might just about have won that election, had Cowley and Headington been included in the constituency, as I had assumed they would be. The truth is, however, that Quintin was a much more effective electioneer than I, certainly on the hustings. On the doorstep, with my more intimate knowledge of the city (after all, I lived there), I might have been his equal. Quintin has always been an exceptional speaker to a large crowd – an orator, to be fair; a demagogue in the minds of his jealous opponents. He is still remembered by old-timers as the chairman who seized a large bell at the Conservative conference and rang it repeatedly amidst the passionate applause of the delegates.

Quintin told me once that his father had said that an

advocate is paid for his opinions, not his doubts. William Jowett, Lord Chancellor when I first joined the Lords, and a superb advocate in his own way, told me, on the other hand, that the secret of advocacy is to find out the worst thing that your opponent can say about your case and say it yourself in your own way. Quintin might be said to belong to the first school, and I, conceivably, to the second. There is no doubt which is the more effective electioneering technique.

Quintin, whose father was Lord Chancellor, was judged academically the most brilliant boy at Eton, where he was Captain of the School. He got a double first at Oxford and won a fellowship at All Souls. When still in his twenties, he won the bitterly-contested Munich by-election in 1938; defeated me (as mentioned) in 1945 and Elizabeth, a better candidate than I, in 1950.

He very nearly became Prime Minister in 1963, having held various high positions. Subsequently he was Lord Chancellor for twelve years – four years under Ted Heath, eight under Margaret Thatcher – a record for this century.

If I were asked who was the most successful boy of my time at Eton I would have to hesitate between him and Alec Home, who defeated him for the premiership in 1963. The bald facts about Quintin, however, give an inadequate picture of the man. Douglas Hurd, for example, was also Captain at Eton and got a double first at Cambridge. I believe he passed first into the diplomatic service. Hurd, like Quintin, came close to being Prime Minister, the winner this time being John Major. It is interesting that in each case the first-class scholar was beaten by a man of limited academic achievement; Alec Home got a third at Oxford, and Major left school at sixteen without, apparently, any O levels.

But the differences are as marked as the resemblances. Douglas Hurd presents a figure of cool distinction, a typical Foreign Office mandarin in the eyes of the public. Quintin is all emotion and irresistible fun. Neither of these qualities has served him well in the ultimate struggle for the leadership but both of them, particularly the second, are the delight of his friends.

He must forgive me for mentioning one particular speech

which tickled me enormously but was received in the House of Lords in silence broken only by his own famous chuckle. He was speaking on a subject concerning the law, and, having recently retired as Mrs Thatcher's Lord Chancellor he could not resist the provocative comment, 'The standards of an honourable profession like the Bar are not quite the same as those of the grocer's shop at the corner of the street in Grantham.' I showed my appreciation, but not many others did.

Douglas Hurd and Quintin Hogg are both religious men; religion has played a large part in Quintin's public and private life. His first wife, a beautiful young woman, left the Catholic Church to marry him and then left him for a Frenchman while Quintin was on active service. His second wife, Mary, provided him with a wonderful family life. He was visibly devastated when she was killed in a riding accident. His third wife, Deirdre, a Catholic whom he married in a Catholic church, has brought him the dignified peace he deserves.

Great affection developed between Quintin and Father D'Arcy. When Father D'Arcy died it was Quintin, close to but not a member of the Catholic Church, who was selected to deliver the address at the requiem at Campion Hall. Those responsible for the choice must have been aware that this would have been in accordance with Father D'Arcy's wishes. It is no good pretending that I was not jealous – far more so than when Quintin defeated me in the by-election.

Although, unlike Quintin, I have never found it easy to speak in public in a fashion which will arouse the enthusiasm of my supporters, I don't believe I have been totally without oratorical skill. To give one example, I once finished winding up a wartime debate for the government in this way:

My lords, I have spoken for longer than I intended. In a few minutes, we will be going into a division. Whatever the result, we in the Government will continue to carry out our responsibilities for the welfare of this country which we all love equally during this very difficult time. Each member of the House will no doubt vote according to his conscience [it was another twelve years before the first women were admitted]. We in the Government will not be found wanting in ours.

I doubt if anyone in the House of Lords talks that way today, but it went down well at the time.

After about a year there was a reshuffle. Clem Attlee, the Prime Minister, sent for me and offered me the position of Parliamentary Secretary to the Minister of National Insurance. As a Beveridge man, I might well have grasped at the chance. I was an obvious choice, as I had been Beveridge's assistant and an improved version of the Beveridge plan was imminent. I accepted automatically, walked along Whitehall – and than asked myself whether there was not some other way of doing something to redeem my failure in the war. It sounds incredible, looking back, but I returned to Downing Street and asked Attlee if I could do something for the Services. He understood my feelings perfectly, in his taciturn way, and at once offered me the position of Under-Secretary of State for War. This gave me a chance to do something at least for the fighting services.

It must be realised that I was now surrounded by generals. Oliver Baldwin, son of the former Prime Minister, befriended me and gave a party for me attended by these same bemedalled generals. He broke the ice in his usual eccentric fashion. 'What I like about the Under-Secretary is that he doesn't pretend to have had a good war record.' Looking round at the top brass: 'Which of you saw service in the front line in the last war?' An embarrassed silence followed. Finally one general plucked up courage to ask, 'Where did you see service in the front line in the last war, Oliver?' 'Eritrea,' he snapped out. No one ventured to say a word after that.

I was also befriended by Monty, as I never called him to his face. At one point, I stayed with him at his mill and was shown the photograph of Rommel which he had I believe kept opposite himself in the desert. He took me down to the staff college at Camberley. Here again, in the larger context, I was the only man in civilian clothes in the middle of the military. Monty finished his address: 'Never forget, gentlemen, the politicians. They are our masters,' pointing to my shrinking figure on the platform. Loud laughter. 'And it's up to us to lead them up the garden path.' Louder laughter.

I can't help casting my mind forward to the moment when Boofy, Earl of Arran, moved an amendment to legalise homosexual behaviour in private between consenting adults – that is, those over twenty-one. Monty called it, not I suppose in public, the Buggers' Charter. In the House, he moved an amendment to permit homosexual behaviour among those over eighty. He reminded the House that he was himself an octogenarian and, at that time of life, not dangerous.

I was speaking effectively in the House at this time, and one speech I made must have attracted the favourable attention of Ernest Bevin, the Foreign Secretary. Germany was in a pitiable condition immediately after the war, and the government were very sensitive to the charge that they were neglecting their duty towards this stricken population. Defending their record, I pronounced, 'Germany today is a tragic mess – but it is a mess of their own making.' Horror-stricken by what I had just said, I ended with a kind of apology. 'May I be forgiven for speaking so about people who are suffering as they are suffering now.'

I think that the first of these remarks rather than the second attracted Bevin. The fact that I was a Catholic may have been a reason for my being chosen as Minister for the British Zone of Germany where the Catholic population formed a high proportion. At any rate, in the spring of 1947 I became Chancellor of the Duchy of Lancaster with responsibility for the British Zone of Germany – in a sense, the high point of my political career.

I was filled with a passionate Christian desire to see justice done to this broken people. I told the schoolchildren of Düsseldorf, desperately hungry, some of them fainting in class, 'Never believe that the whole world is against you; you're absolutely right to be proud of being German.' Good words then and now; unfortunately, that was not the policy of the Allies at the time – Allies including not only the USA and France, but the Soviet Union.

When I returned to England I was asked by the Foreign Office whether I minded being accompanied by a PR on my next visit who could (though they did not say it quite like that) plane away my more dangerous utterances.

There was a good deal of pleasure among the Control Commission in the British Zone that a minister was taking such a strong personal interest. But the attitude of the Military Governor, General Brian Robertson, was at that time, guarded. A strong Christian like his son, the present Lord Robertson, who is a brave spokesman in the Lords, the General may have had more sympathy for my point of view than he showed. But it was his business to apply the official policy of the British government, not that of the young idealist whose tenure, for all he knew, was precarious.

In practice he was of much assistance to the Germans in those painful times. I remember a memorandum of his which began, 'Without food nothing can happen' – and the flow of fresh supplies which immediately followed. Two years later when I was visiting Dr Adenauer, in my capacity of Minister of Civil Aviation, the German Chancellor expressed extreme regret at the departure of Brian Robertson. But by that time British official policy, under the Russian threat, had become much more friendly to the Germans.

I recall one glorious moment in my time as Minister for the British Zone. I was attending the Buckingham Palace garden party in 1947, when Winston Churchill, then Leader of the Opposition, stumped across to speak to me. 'I am glad', he spelt out slowly as always, 'that there is one mind suffering for the miseries of Germany.' He paused to improve the phrasing. 'One English mind suffering for the miseries of Germany.' For once, I forbore to point out that I consider myself an Irishman.

I did not possess the strength of character to live up to my aspirations. As I have already mentioned, I sent more than one offer of resignation during the following months to Clem Attlee, quite long letters, springing from a tortured conscience. His replies were friendly but terse.

Not until much later did I discover what Attlee really felt about the Germans. When we were seeing a lot of each other in the House of Lords and I was chairman of the

Anglo–German Association, I asked Clem to be a patron. He paused, because he did not like causing pain, but felt bound to tell me, 'You ought to know that I have always disliked the Germans. Vi and I had a German maid we were very fond of – but she was an exception.'

Meanwhile I dashed backwards and forwards to Germany twenty-six times in the years. I came to know leading German politicians quite well, including Dr Adenauer. I was helpful to him on one occasion when, for the first time, Germans were allowed to take part in an international conference in The Hague. I asked him afterwards how he got on with Churchill, then Leader of the Opposition. Adenauer replied, 'In the hour of my nation's humiliation, I did not press myself on him.' Which brought to my mind Churchill saying of the Germans, 'They are either at your throat or at your feet.' In fact a relationship was initiated between Adenauer and Churchill which bore fruit later.

I am tempted to digress with an anecdote somewhat out of place, since it happened in 1953. Churchill, then Prime Minister, entertained Chancellor Adenauer at a dinner at Downing Street. I was invited, as chairman of the Anglo–German Association. Monty was standing by me after dinner; Churchill came lumbering round to talk to his guests. Monty, putting on a tough soldierly act, pointed to my hair, which was long at the sides though non-existent, even then, on top. 'Don't you think he needs his hair cutting, PM?' asked Monty. Churchill surveyed him coolly and then, speaking very slowly, replied, 'Your head, my dear Field Marshal, requires compression under a military cap. He needs his for speaking in the House of Lords.'

To return to my performance as Minister for the British Zone, I am still glad I said all those things, and still cannot make up my mind whether I should have forced through my resignation. During that year, 1947–8, I was closer to the centre of the highest policy-making than ever before; closer than I was later, as a member of the cabinet.

At the end of 1947 the Council of Foreign Ministers met for three weeks in London under the chairmanship of Ernest Bevin. I sat at his elbow throughout. One day, when he was unwell, I actually presided. There came a moment when General Marshall, the American Secretary of State, became so infuriated with the negativism of Mr Molotov, the Soviet Minister, whom I sat next to, that he announced it was no good going on. Bevin for the first and last time asked my advice – should he also agree to terminate the conference?

I suggested that he should defer his decision to the morning, knowing how desperately anxious he was not to break the world into the two halves, West and East. The matter however was taken out of his hands. Bidault, the French Foreign Minister, sided with Marshall, so Bevin had to accept the ending of the conference. Next day he kept returning to the same questions. He was still unhappy at the break. It did not hold him back, however, from taking the initiative which led to the formation of the historic Atlantic Alliance.

During the conference, I was a guest at a very enjoyable dinner party at the Russian embassy given in honour of Mr Molotov. The ladies were segregated at one end of the table, so I found myself next to the guest of honour. Molotov, his eyes glittering behind pince-nez, asked me in his usual courteous fashion, 'Have you studied Karl Marx, Lord Pakenham?' I replied that I had not only studied him but lectured on him at Oxford. I was afraid, however, that I was not a Marxist. Molotov, still courteous, replied (all through the interpreter), 'I could not expect to find a good Marxist in the House of Lords.'

Bevin, on the other side of me, cut in, 'That's where you're wrong, Mr Molotov; the Lords are the only people in England who have time to read Karl Marx.' Molotov, still apparently unruffled, suggested that Mr Bevin should read Karl Marx in the commentary of Hilferding. Bevin was not to be defeated. 'I've read Hilferding,' he retorted, though it's difficult to believe he had, 'and I found him tedious.'

There came a time in the summer of 1948 when I was laid up with a broken Achilles tendon, sustained in the last serious game of squash I ever played. Attlee called on me at our house in Golders Green and asked me to become Minister of Civil Aviation. Technically and financially it was a promotion, though much less significant in European politics. 'I think it's time you had your own department,' he said, adding the seductive inducement, 'Christopher Addison can't go on for ever.' (Addison was Leader of the House of Lords.) I allowed myself to be 'kicked upstairs'. After all these years, I still don't known whether that was an honourable way out.

I will add here a meeting with Dr Adenauer after I had ceased to have responsibility for Germany. As Minister of Civil Aviation I called on Adenauer in 1950, when he and Schumann, the French PM, were initiating what afterwards became the European Economic Community. He begged me to go back to Attlee and Bevin and try to persuade them to join France and Germany at that crucial point in history. I still do not know whether he thought I had any influence at such a level of policy. In fact I had none. I did my best, but not surprisingly got nowhere. At that time, a high official in the Treasury wrote a memo saying that to join Europe would be to tie us to a corpse.

14
THE ZEALOUS
MINISTER
1948–51

From mid 1948 to the end of 1951 I was a departmental minister outside the cabinet: for three years Minister of Civil Aviation; for six months First Lord of the Admiralty, in the days when such a position still existed. I would have said that I made a considerable impact in the former role, none at all in the latter, although I had a happy and glorious time in that office, including residence with my family in Admiralty House.

I was equally ignorant of aeroplanes and ships, but that was not unusual in those days. I was in my early forties when I became Minister of Civil Aviation, and full of reforming zeal. I was faced with the fact that the three corporations – BOAC, BEA and BSAA – were operating at a considerable loss. I took a very tough line, and swiftly introduced new chairmen at BOAC and BEA, and amalgamated BSAA with BOAC. Looking back I find my younger self rather brutal, or at least insensitive.

The chairman of BOAC was a distinguished scientist, somewhat crippled by lameness but much respected. We in the ministry (though I, of course, was responsible) decided that he must be replaced. Whether by accident of not, he set off just then on a world tour. When he returned he invited me to dinner at the Dorchester. He dwelt at some length on the pleasures of maturity. 'I don't worry now,' he said, 'like I did when I was a younger man.' I brought these happy thoughts to an end by asking how old he was. He replied, 'I am in my seventieth year', which to me sounded impossibly old. When I broke the news to him that his time was up, he looked ten or more years older. I still think that I probably did the right thing, but not in the right way.

The staff of each corporation was rapidly reduced without a reduction of flying time. The finances greatly improved. All this was easier in a new industry. One could reduce staff by the simple expedient of not taking on new entrants. On the face of it, I did a good job as a minister. I owed much to the drive and efficiency of the two chairmen I appointed, Sir Miles Thomas (BOAC) and Marshal of the Royal Air Force, Sir Sholto Douglas (BEA), whose appointment was greeted in the Press with the cry 'jobs for the boys' when he took his seat on the Labour bench in the House of Lords. Their approaches were totally different. One, that of the motor industry, the other that of an ex-fighter pilot. Both were equally inspiring and successful.

But pride so often comes before a fall. After I had been minister for eighteen months there was a report on the fatal crash at Prestwick, near Glasgow. The official inquiry blamed my traffic controllers. My ministry experts advised me to set it aside, which I did with some éclat. There was a terrific outcry. Someone said to my uncle Arthur Villiers, 'I say, Arthur, this nephew of yours seems a regular Mussolini.' Clem Attlee, for the only time in my experience, was positively hostile. Had I consulted any senior minister before taking this step, which had caused the government a lot of trouble in the Commons? The papers alternated between the headlines 'PAKENHAM MUST GO' and 'PAKENHAM IS GOING'. They never got quite as far as saying, 'PAKENHAM HAS GONE', but it must have been touch and go. The aeroplane in question was Dutch (KLM), and the Dutch inquiry later put all the blame on their pilot, so in that sense I was vindicated. But I learnt a lesson not easily forgotten. If you are a member of a government you can't act entirely on your own. You are relying on others. They must be able to rely on you.

It will be recalled that when I was 'promoted' to Civil Aviation, Attlee had said that Addison, Leader of the Lords, couldn't last for ever. But my prospects had been seriously damaged. I was happily surprised in May 1951 when Attlee sent for me and said, 'I want you to be First Lord of the Admiralty.' Although I was yearning for promotion I felt unexpectedly diffident. I blurted out, 'I feel I am too eccentric.' Attlee dismissed that difficulty. 'The Navy', he said, 'has survived Winston and Brendan Bracken. It will probably survive you.' Which was true of the Navy, but not true for long of the Admiralty as an independent department.

I was treated with infinite kindness and courtesy by the admirals. I did not feel, however, that anything I could do or say would have much effect on such a wonderfully organised traditional structure. I presided over the Board of Admiralty. Lord Mountbatten, on the way back from being Supreme Commander in South East Asia and Viceroy of India, was no higher than Fourth Sea Lord. On one occasion he argued rather strongly for a transfer to his department of some of the functions of the First Sea Lord. The latter, though older than Mountbatten, had served under him in SEAC. 'You look after your department, young fella m'lad,' he said to Mountbatten, 'and I'll look after mine.' I admired Mountbatten's self-control. 'If that's how you put it, sir, I bow to your superior stripes.' Frazer, the First Sea Lord, was instantly mollified. ' Not a bit of it, my dear boy,' he said. 'We're all equal at the Board of Admiralty.' Which of course was completely untrue in practice. Certainly the First Lord, myself, was not more equal than the others.

In November 1951 a general election swept the Labour government from power and me with it. Later, I gave a brief account of my time at the Admiralty in something I wrote. Mountbatten wrote to me, 'If I had known more of your background I could have helped you more.' I shall always think of him as an enormously helpful man, particularly to Elizabeth when she was writing about the Royal House of Windsor. She sent him the proofs of her book. He was embarking on a world tour, but sent back the annotated proofs whenever he touched land.

During these years I made many speeches from the Opposition front bench in the Lords. I recall with pleasure the fact that, much assisted by Herbert Morrison, Deputy Prime

Minister, I made a powerful defence of Voluntary Action in 1949, at a time when the Labour government's attitude to it was somewhat obscure. 'Voluntary Action', I cried, 'is the life blood of democracy. Without Voluntary Action democracy loses its soul.' I cannot help thinking that that speech was something of a turning point in the attitude of the Labour government to Voluntary Action.

I have mentioned elsewhere my rather feeble protest before the cabinet about government policy when Ireland left the Commonwealth. Also my vain efforts in 1950 to suggest that the government should take a more active interest in the beginnings of the European idea.

By 1951 I would have said that, in the eyes of the authorities, I was a youngish politician not to be ignored, but with a question mark hanging over my future.

I owe so much to Clem Attlee that the least I can offer in return is a few reflections here. Physically small, ever smaller as the years passed, and unobtrusive-looking, Attlee was, as I have called him in the Lords, an ethical giant. It is true that when asked, 'Are you a Christian, Lord Attlee?' he replied, 'Accept the Christian ethic, can't stand the mumbo-jumbo.' But his formation was strongly Christian; his best friends, as he told his fine biographer Kenneth Harris, were Christian and, above all, his brother Tom, a Christian pacifist, remained a supreme influence. He never mentioned my father to me, but I have always believed that my father's having died at Gallipoli, where Attlee also served, gave him a special interest in me.

I did not have the advantage of having been educated at Attlee's school, Haileybury, like Chris Mayhew, but I was by and large the public-school mission type which Attlee well understood, having as a young man served for many years in the East End himself. I always felt that that East End background had given him an assured place in the hearts of the Labour Party, which no one else drawn from the upper-middle classes could quite attain to.

The story of his relationship with Dick Crossman, generally regarded as the most brilliant of my generation of Socialists, is a sad one. Dick's father, a judge, had played tennis with Clem as a boy, later recalling unkindly Attlee's 'waspish inaccuracy' at the net. Attlee never liked Dick's attitude to his father. Dick had been head of Winchester and on the face of it might have appealed to Clem Attlee, but in the event he wrote him off as having no judgement. Dick never received any appointment under him, even the humblest. He had to wait till his late fifties before he achieved office.

Was Attlee at fault here? Did he miss the chance of using somebody who might have done great things for causes to which he himself had dedicated his life? It is possible to think so, but I do not think that way myself.

Dick Crossman had immense potential. Not only had he been awarded a philosophy fellowship at New College when he took his final exams, but he was a splendid physical specimen; as we soon discovered when he played for our rugger club at Aylesbury, he was not only big and strong, but distinctly fast. And he had considerable powers of leadership. On one occasion I asked him to take over the leadership of the rugby pack. Clapping his hands, with a 'Come on, chaps' he reanimated them superbly.

In his Coventry constituency before the war, the working-class looked upon Crossman as a sort of Messiah. I have never listened to more powerful lectures than those he gave in the schools on Nazi Germany in the late thirties. But one has to admit there were reasons other than the easy pun for his acquiring the title 'Double Crossman' early in the day. The Oxford wit who described Crossman as a *L'Attaque* piece got it all wrong. He could never be frightened into changing sides. The current jibe was truer; that if you went for a walk with Dick, he forced you to agree with an unlikely proposition in the first half-hour, and to a still more unlikely opposite in the second.

I may be a suspect witness here. In his diaries he has referred to me as a farcical figure in the cabinet, but diaries are diaries. One must not take the entries too seriously. When I took up the cause of pornography, or rather anti-pornography, the *New Statesman*, of which by that time Dick was editor again, accorded me a front-page leading article under the heading 'Full Frontal Hypocrisy'. Dick was not in the least embarrassed when I met him soon afterwards. He assured me glibly that the article would do me nothing but good.

Roy Jenkins concludes, in his essay on Dick in his *Selected Writings*, 'In later life, I did not exactly admire him, but I enjoyed his company to an extent matched by only three or four other politicians.' Elizabeth was fonder of him than I was, but we both found him a great enhancer of life. Clem Attlee clearly felt differently. Perhaps the difference between them might be attributed partly to their politics. Dick Crossman was generally thought to be further to the Left than Attlee. On the other hand, the Oxford City Labour Party, which I was so involved with, were vehemently left-wing, but I never heard any criticism of Clem Attlee. The first time I appeared with him in public was at a meeting in Oxford town hall to celebrate the resignation of Antony Eden from the Chamberlain cabinet in 1938. Clem was not very well at the time; he and I spent some time in the lavatory, where we could hear the crowd becoming impatient. Clem, in his quiet yet effective way, rose to the occasion, and was carried in triumph round Oxford. Hugh Fraser, my future son-in-law, and other anti-Chamberlain Conservatives emerged from the Carlton Club to join in the fun.

After my defeat at Oxford, I was surprised to receive a letter from Attlee congratulating me on the fight I had put up and asking me to go to the Lords and become a Lord-in-Waiting (a junior ministerial post). A year later, after I had spoken (looking back, it seems almost incessantly) from the Labour front bench in the Lords, came the reshuffle I have spoken of, in which Clem, as I never dared to call him, asked me to go to the Ministry of National Insurance, then concurred with my wish to do something for the Services, and appointed me Under-Secretary for War.

I have already explained what a strain I placed on Attlee's patience when I was Minister for Germany, and how kind he was to me. I blotted my copybook by my handling of the Prestwick crash, which I suppose was inept. But when I was First Lord of the Admiralty I seemed to regain his confidence. When he came to the House of Lords, we were almost like father and son. His last great cause was World Government, in which I backed him up devotedly.

Clem Attlee combined humility and self-esteem in a fashion that I have never seen equalled. One evening, after a debate in the Lords, he and Vi asked Elizabeth and me to join them at dinner. Rather embarrassed, he admitted he knew no restaurants nearby, so I nominated the Queen's Restaurant just off Sloane Square as reputable but inexpensive. When dinner was over, after a muttered colloquy with Vi, he explained to me, 'These people won't know who I am' (he was already ex-Prime Minister, an Earl, KG, OM). 'Would you mind giving them your cheque, and I will give you mine?'

But he could stand on his rights as well as any man. We used to accord him the first seat below the gangway on the ministerial side of the house. One day he came in rather late and found it occupied by a portly colleague. Clem stood in front of him, without saying a word, until the portly one moved along.

Clem Attlee had exceptionally high moral standards, which he communicated by example rather than precept. I will leave him to write his own epitaph:

> *They said he wasn't a starter,*
> *There were many who thought themselves smarter,*
> *But they made him PM, PC and OM,*
> *An Earl and a Knight of the Garter!*

15
BANKING AND
PRISONERS
1951–64

In these thirteen 'wasted' years, to use the Labour Party's description, I was involved in innumerable activities in the outside world but they did not constitute my whole life. Towards the end of the period Elizabeth laid the foundations of her enduring fame as a pre-eminent historian with her books on the Jameson Raid and Queen Victoria. My eight children, if a plagiarism from St Luke is forgiven, 'advanced in strength and wisdom and in favour with God and man'. By 1964 the last of my four sons was on the point of leaving Ampleforth; Antonia had already made her literary mark, Judith and Rachel would soon be making theirs. My religious life had struggled forward.

Soon after the Labour government fell, my staunch friends Hugh Trevor-Roper, now Lord Dacre, and Robert (now Lord) Blake took pity on my position out of work and invited me back to Christ Church as a full member of the governing body, teaching only two days a week. I made a lasting friend in Roger Opie, then on a Rhodes Scholarship from Adelaide. He came to visit me in my 'consulting room' in Brewer Street, beginning with the words, 'Do you keep a shotgun behind the door?' This was his charming Australian way of paying tribute to the attractions of Antonia, whom he had just met in the passage. Later he assisted me with my work on the causes of crime, in the course of which I introduced him to Norma

Canter, with the happiest possible consequences, including three delightful children. When I last met her, Norma was teaching mathematics, which shows how little one realises the potentialities of glamorous young women.

Nigel Lawson was my pupil for politics, his third subject in philosophy, politics and economics. He was referred to in those days as the most brilliant young philosopher among the undergraduates. Since then, he has been Chancellor of the Exchequer for a longer period than anyone except Lloyd George. It would be impertinent for me to criticise his political skills. Nevertheless, if he had asked my advice (which he was a hundred miles from doing) he would not have supported Michael Heseltine when he stood for leadership of the Conservative Party. Nigel had already antagonised the Thatcherites; he now seemed surprised that the supporters of John Major who had served under Nigel in the Treasury were equally affronted. However, even the most brilliant men are not always worldly wise.

In 1954 I was approached out of the blue and asked whether I would become chairman of the National Bank at the beginning of 1955, learning the trade for the rest of 1954 as deputy chairman. It may be asked how on earth I came to be selected, with no previous experience in banking. I had, admittedly, attained a first in Philosophy, Politics and Economics, specialising in banking and currency, but I doubt if the formidable Mr Cook, the chairman about to retire, knew of that qualification or would have been interested. I had, too, been Labour Party Treasury spokesman for six years in the Lords. If he knew of that I doubt if he would have approved of it. Both in my time and since, retiring Conservative ministers have been fitted out with excellent jobs in the City, but for a Socialist my appointment created a precedent which has not so far been repeated.

In my nine years in the City, 1954 to 1963, I lunched there almost every day; I never met anyone of remotely Labour Party sympathies at those lunches – nor did I ever meet a woman. Would it be much different today? Not very, in the case of the Socialists; a little, but not much different in the case of women. During the half century in which I have functioned in the

Lords, I can think of only four Labour colleagues who knew much about the City – Harold Lever, Bernard Donoghue, Clive Hollick and Charles Williams; and of these only Charles, once managing director of Barings, had worked at what I would call its real centre.

It is, however, not difficult to understand why I was selected. The National Bank was a strange, anomalous, if you like anachronistic entity by the time I became its chairman. Founded by Daniel O'Connell in the 1830s, it possessed more branches in Ireland than any other bank but its headquarters were in England, where it only had about thirteen branches.

We possessed an honoured position as one of the smaller clearing banks. Every month I attended a meeting of the eleven clearing chairmen, where, in theory at least, I was the equal of my mentor Anthony Tuke, chairman of Barclay's, an old Wykehamist. I remember him telling me that if you wanted to make a lot of money you would not become a bank chairman. He was not sure whether he could really afford a full-time gardener.

Today the chairman of Barclay's is I gather paid a great deal, but recent losses would have made Anthony Tuke turn in his grave. I was paid £5,000 a year, which I was also paid when I became a cabinet minister soon afterwards. A short time later again that figure was raised to £8,500.

It is no good pretending that I was popular with the powers that were in the City. I was put up for the City Club with impeccable backing, but comprehensively blackballed. 'I love Frank,' one member was overheard to say, 'but I am not going to have him coming in here and getting all the advantages of the City [sic] when he and his lot want to smash it all up.'

I do not regard this as an idiotic reaction. It would be a libel to say that those who give their lives to their work in the City are interested only in moneymaking. When it comes to raising money for charities, these people are remarkably responsive. Besides, I have a close example in my son Kevin, the first member of my family since Arthur Villiers to succeed in the City. Kevin obtained a higher degree in economics, has travelled all over the world, and is intellectually absorbed in international problems. No one who looks at the reality of

Britain's position and the creation of wealth which we all depend on can doubt the enormous value of the City of London to the standard of life of the British people. It does not follow, of course, that because a large institution is valuable its views should predominate, but they should never be neglected. Those who work there are neither better nor worse than the rest of us.

I had, I have to admit, an exceptionally agreeable time. In a sense I feel that I have never left the National Bank. Every year I go to meetings of the pensioners and we glory in our reminiscences. Being much smaller than today's Big Five banks, we claimed to provide a much more human service. Whether this would still have been possible with the coming of the computer I cannot say. Today one is asked for one's number rather than one's name, and may be told that no such number is known to the computer. What made my task easier was that my predecessor Mr Cook, a character if ever there was one, brought up in the hard school of a branch in southern Ireland, had adopted a very restrictive attitude to staff salaries. He had warned me, incidentally, never to let any single member of staff know *everything*. The accountancy branch, for example, should report only to me. Mr Cook's approach to life can be illustrated by two anecdotes. When I became deputy chairman he was still presiding, and a 'go-slow' strike was in operation in the Irish branches. The villain of the piece in our eyes was a Mr Titterington, the Trades Union official over there. On one occasion the Irish directors joined us and were subjected to a withering blast of criticism from Mr Cook. They seemed unable to reply. In exasperation he opened a drawer in the boardroom table and pulled out an ancient pistol. 'Take that,' he told these senior gentlemen from Ireland. 'It should give you the spunk to cope with Mr Titterington.'

One of our London directors had been the last governor of the Punjab, and had been found a position in our bank by the Governor of the Bank of England. Constructively minded after his long experience of ruling millions, he produced a plan to reorganise the National Bank. My dear friend and private secretary, Peggy Fitzgerald, told me of the scene that followed. Mr Cook picked up this well-considered memorandum and told the ex-governor, 'Do you know what I think of your proposals? This.' And he tore them into shreds.

It was not difficult to ingratiate myself with the staff after their rough handling by Mr Cook. I swiftly announced my determination that they should be paid as well as staff in other banks. I visited every branch in England and, I like to think, every branch, however remote, in Ireland.

Churchill said during the war, 'I was not the lion's heart. I was the lion's roar.' There was a deep feeling of comradeship in the National Bank in Ireland and in England. I was privileged to give it expression. At the end of my time I was described in the *Economist* as being 'vastly successful'. Our business in England increased three times as fast as the average of the banks.

The staff gave me a Mini car as a leaving testimonial. I am not sure whether they knew that I couldn't drive. I was determined to prove worthy of them. While Elizabeth was in America for a fortnight I took intensive lessons. A date for a driving test was fixed, but on the last day I backed into a sapling in our drive and lowered it to the ground. Our gardener removed all traces. But Elizabeth's first question on her return was, 'Where is the sapling?' I threw my hand in and have never attempted to drive a car again. Maybe that is the reason why at eighty-eight I can still jog (very slowly) for two or three miles.

Mary Craig, in her usual balanced way, says that any attempt on my part to bring the City and the Labour Party closer together failed. That is undeniably true. I am not sure whether I ever entertained any very serious hopes of such an initiative succeeding. Rothschilds alone of the leading City firms I knew encouraged me to bring eminent Socialists there. I remember taking Frank Cousins and Aneurin Bevan to lunch there. We were told that John Smith, in whom I had a special confidence as the Leader of the Labour Party, made an excellent impression in the City. I hoped then that he would be an octogenarian before he ceased to lead our Party, but it unfortunately has to be said that it was never likely that he would be offered the chairmanship of a major bank.

One final comment on banking. During the eight years

while I was chairman of the bank there were six chancellors of the exchequer, all Conservative. By coincidence, during six out of the eight years we were subjected to controls, in that we were asked to restrain our lending, with a clear indication that if we did not conform the Bank of England would know how to bring us to book. Thirty years later we are told that controls of that kind – imposed, I repeat, under Conservative rule – have become impossible.

1954 was a significant year for me in more ways than one. I was lucky indeed to be asked by the Nuffield Foundation to undertake an inquiry into the causes of crime. My expert assessors were of the highest quality, all eminent: two psychiatrists, a sociologist, a stipendiary magistrate and the director of the Foundation. The report was later published over my name.

My disappearance into banking terminated the work before the Foundation considered that the ground had been fully covered. It cannot be said that we provided very definite answers to the question, What causes crime? But then the same can be said of all who have attempted the task before or since. My old friend Dr John Bowlby laid his emphasis on maternal deprivation in the first two years, or even the first six months of life as a principal cause of crime. I remember Frank Milton, our stipendiary magistrate, explaining his reasons before leaving one of our meetings. 'I have to go and sentence', he said, 'a fraudulent company promoter who no doubt lacked affection in his first few months of life.'

In the end we placed our main emphasis on the broken home. By 1994 we are all too well aware that the numbers of broken homes have vastly increased since the 1950s. We listed, however, a large number of other factors which might increase the risk of crime.

In 1955 I opened the first debate on prisons ever held in the House of Lords.

At the same time, I was following an intensive programme of visiting prisons and prisoners. I suppose the two best known prisoners I visited at that time were George Blake and Christopher Craig. George Blake, with his black beard, convicted of spying, struck me as the most foreign-looking man I had ever seen. I could not understand how he had ever been recruited for any form of the Secret Service, but he was full of charm and in something I wrote soon afterwards I said that I hoped 'to be of service to him some time'. He averted that possibility by making a sensational escape in which, I hasten to say, I played no part. I became friendly with his mother, a Dutchwoman, and his then wife, a lady of impeccable antecedents.

Christopher Craig is remembered nowadays because of his connection with Derek Bentley. Craig, then a boy of under sixteen, shot a policeman. Bentley, mentally subnormal, was supposed to have shouted, 'Let him have it, Chris.' Bentley was hanged; surely the most deliberately outrageous decision ever taken by a Home Secretary. Yet the Home Secretary was a man of honourable character, which only goes to show the distortions of conduct that can occur when capital punishment is permitted.

I got to know Christopher Craig quite well in prison. He was, incidentally, dyslexic and learnt in prison to read and write. When he was set free, I was in the cabinet. He asked me to his wedding. I am still ashamed to think that I shirked the occasion. The Prime Minister, Harold Wilson, with his tiny majority in the Commons, expressed the hope that I would not attend, though he had never been unfriendly to penal reform. Weakly, I gave way, and tried to salve my conscience by asking Christopher and his fiancée to dinner the night before the wedding. Looking back, that failure to go to the wedding, and my decision to stand as Labour candidate in Oxford in 1939, are the two political actions I regret most.

Also in 1955, with the help of others, I started the New Bridge for ex-prisoners, which has flourished increasingly from that day to this. As I write these lines I am about to go to the memorial service of Jane Ewart-Biggs, chairman of the society for five years till her health gave way. Jane was loved by all. There was deep sympathy for her after the assassination of her husband, but she made a personal mark that was all her own. The New Bridge is today in exceptionally capable hands with Peter, Lord Henderson, as president and Eric McGraw as director, and is in very good standing with the Home Office. It was not always so.

When we began, we were closely associated with the 'three musketeers', three notable young men who had been sent to prison for relatively minor homosexual offences. (One of them claims that he devised the name of New Bridge. Victor Gollancz, another great champion of prisoners, among others, made a similar claim.) Our first secretary was admittedly gay, to use the modern word, and someone in the Home Office put it about that we were a group of homosexuals catering for fellow homosexuals. Someone is supposed to have said, 'Lord Longford has eight children,' to which the official is supposed to have replied, 'Oh, that's just a cover.'

By the time a Labour government was formed in 1964 I was quite well known, according to my personal assistant at the time, Angela Lambert, since then highly successful as journalist, television producer and novelist, as 'that prison person'. When the Labour government was formed, Evelyn Waugh, whose friendship for me never restrained his tongue, wrote to Lady Donaldson, 'I'm glad Frank won't be Home Secretary, otherwise we should all have been murdered in our beds.'

As a Labour spokesman in the Lords I was active and loyal, but in view of my bank chairmanship my total contribution was less than that of some others. Our leader very soon became Albert (Earl) Alexander, a former Minister of Defence from the Commons. He was a devoted Christian, but not quite my kind of Christian. In fact, he was an extremely old-fashioned Baptist. He would pull out his Bible and read the New Testament aloud to me on the front bench – 'a sacrifice not to be repeated, not to be repeated, Frank – how do you explain that?' I was saved by the loud cries of Order! Order! from all over the chamber.

There was one occasion when we both left our front bench seats and spoke from the back benches. Boofy (Earl of Arran) introduced a motion in favour of Christian unity. Everyone in the House was in favour of the impending visit of the Archbishop of Canterbury, Geoffrey Fisher, to Rome, except Albert. He interrupted Archbishop Fisher repeatedly, finally putting what seemed to him the unanswerable question, 'Which is the Church of England, Protestant or Catholic?' Fisher gave him the superior smile of a former headmaster. 'Both,' he replied sweetly. Albert was left expostulating vainly.

But morality interested Albert even more than theology. One day a Catholic peer was talking about the immorality of sex outside marriage. Albert turned to Jack Lawson, another doughty non-conformist beside him. 'You know, Jack, these Catholics are the only non-conformists left.'

By 1964, no one could question my fidelity to the Party, or general powers of spokesmanship. But Albert, who was much older than I – though not as old as I am now – could be forgiven for thinking that he had prior claims to the leadership of the Lords if Labour came back to power.

To my gratification, I had been elected a member of the Other Club, the select dining club founded by Churchill and Birkenhead shortly before the 1914 War. I may have been the statutory Socialist, but I was delighted to be asked to join.

Winston Churchill by that time had lost most of his memory. He seemed to recognise no one except the other new member, Onassis, on whose yacht he had recently been staying. I was placed opposite Churchill during dinner, during which he looked at me blankly. There came a moment, however, when a beautiful smile crossed his face. He leaned across and raised his champagne glass to me. Millions of men and women have happy memories of Churchill, whether they have known him or not. That is the happiest of mine.

16
IMPOTENT GLORY

No cabinet has ever contained such a high proportion of first-class academics as the one Wilson formed in 1964. We included five Oxford dons: Wilson, Crossman, Gordon Walker, Crosland and myself. Four other members of the cabinet had received first-class degrees at Oxford: Jay, a Fellow of All Souls; Stewart, a President of the Union; Jenkins, now Chancellor of Oxford; and Healey, the most rounded intellectual of the politicians in my time, counting in his music and painting.

Asquith's cabinet, it may be said, paraded more notable personalities – Asquith himself, Lloyd George, Gray, Churchill and Haldane. So, it might be argued, did the Attlee cabinet which included Bevin, Cripps, Dalton, Morrison and Bevan. But academically we set a record which is not likely to be challenged. From one particular point of view Douglas Jay and Roy Jenkins (the latter of a younger generation) provide an intriguing contrast. Both are highly qualified intellectually; both are men of unquestionable integrity; but from early days they took up sharply opposed attitudes towards the issue of Europe. I can remember a fringe debate between them at the Labour conference in 1962. Roy certainly jeopardised his relationship with his leader Hugh Gaitskell by his passionate Europeanism, though the breach was healed before Hugh died.

Since then Roy Jenkins, having been a Labour Chancellor of

the Exchequer, has left the Party. He presided for a time over the Social Democrats, which he did so much to found, and is now Liberal Democratic Leader in the Lords. When I 'twitted' him in a debate for having far surpassed my own record of tergiversation, having been a Leader of three parties within a short space of time, he replied that he had always maintained the same general position, that of a Social Democrat. Today he sits in the Lords next to Mark Bonham Carter, incidentally one of the sharpest speakers in the House, who also imagines, I would think, that he has never changed his general position.

In the debates on Maastricht recently, Roy and our very capable Leader Ivor Richard fought shoulder-to-shoulder in favour of the Treaty. Douglas, whose own cabinet career was terminated in 1967 by his anti-Europe posture, maintained a heart-and-soul opposition to the official line of the party of which he has remained a dedicated member.

Another comparison is inevitable, between those two long-time friends and rivals, Tony Crosland and Roy Jenkins. I am not very observant of masculine beauty, but Tony Crosland was good-looking by any standards. Did his combination of exceptional brain and physical charm produce a certain superciliousness, as his detractors alleged? I remember an occasion when he told me, in friendly fashion, that I would have had much more influence on his generation if I had not been so arrogant in my attitude towards the waiters in the George Café, Oxford. I said to myself, 'Well, well, well!' But Tony gave immense pleasure, not all of it intellectual, to his many friends. His death at the age of fifty-eight (F.E. Smith died at the same age, as did my brother) was a tragic blow for his much admired wife Susan.

Roy Jenkins, in a slightly different fashion, has developed a certain grandeur of style. A few will remember his family in Wales, and regret the disappearance of any trace of a Welsh accent, but I unreservedly salute him as he is. I sometimes wonder whether he is more like Dilke or Asquith (on both of whom he has written successful books), or Gladstone, on whom he is at the moment preparing a magnum opus. But why not George Nathaniel Curzon, one of his predecessors as Chancellor of Oxford University, a Balliol man like himself and the original of Belloc's 'Most Superior Person'? Churchill has paid tribute to his book *Invincible Humour*. Birkenhead, another good judge, obviously thought highly of him also; I remember his unveiling a bust of Curzon in the Oxford Union and affectionately assuring us, 'No one would have enjoyed our ceremony more than George Curzon.' Roy has written all too generously about myself, more deservedly about Elizabeth. He has written of me that the causes or subjects I take up 'will not always be chosen with perfect discrimination, but they will certainly be pursued with a unique combination of courage, zest and wit'. I would say of him that he represents the best kind of contemporary civilisation more perfectly than anyone I know and deserves every atom of the great success that has come his way, including the OM.

The Wilson cabinet of 1964–8 has not up till now won many plaudits. Statistics, as we know, can be used to prove many things; they can certainly be used to demonstrate that our record was as good as that of any other post-war cabinet. But, as so many Labour governments have found, the best laid plans can be sabotaged by a run on the pound.

On the first day we met in 1964 we were told at the end of business by Jim Callaghan, Chancellor of the Exchequer, 'You will be glad to hear that the pound has had a good day.' In 1966 came one devaluation crisis, in 1967 another, which led ultimately to my resignation. Since then the present government has had its Black Wednesday.

I am not pretending that the problem will ever be totally disposed of. Going deeper, I would suggest that this greatly gifted team of Socialists had not yet come to grips with the problem of making capitalism work. There will be no easy answers but, in a later chapter, I will explain my reasons for my confidence in the present leaders of the Labour Party.

I suppose MPs and parliamentary candidates would say that the most nerve-racking moments they have experienced were those spent waiting for the returning officer to declare the results at an election. Tucked away in the House of Lords from 1945, I had not enjoyed that experience, but I had an anxious time during the twenty-four hours following the Labour victory in 1964. I came up to London and waited for what seemed an interminable time in our flat. Eventually the telephone rang and I was on my way to Downing Street.

Harold greeted me in kindly fashion. In his eyes, I suppose, I was an unreconstructed Gaitskellite, but then and later, even under distressing circumstances, he never showed me anything but kindness. 'I want you to be Leader of the House,' he said, 'of course a member of the cabinet and Lord Privy Seal. I should have liked you to be the Lord President of the Council, but I am told that he has to be in the House of Commons.' I did not stop to ask myself who told him that. I accepted with outstretched hands. He added, a shade mischievously, 'There was another claimant', whom he named, 'but I consulted Clem Attlee who said it had to be you.' There was never anyone outside my family whose approval I valued more than that of Clem Attlee.

A Leader of the House of Lords has three connected functions. He is maître d'hotel, government spokesman, and participant in the formation of government policy. Through my misfortune or my fault, I played little part under the last heading. In a book about the decline of the aristocracy, I have been referred to as a 'feeble' member of the cabinet. Cecil King, in one of his diaries (published incidentally by my subsequent firm, Sidgwick & Jackson), quotes Harold Wilson as saying that I had the mentality of a boy of twelve. Wilson later explained that this had been a misunderstanding. 'No, I did not say that. I may have said that he had the judgement of a twelve-year-old or, better still, the innocence, but he had a very fine brain.'

Harold Wilson was, however, well aware that I was very disappointed not to be in charge of any government committees, as other Leaders of the House have been.

It's true [agrees Sir Harold] that a Lord Privy Seal is expected to chair committees. But I couldn't have used Frank like that, because senior ministers didn't take him seriously enough. He was too off-beat. He's a crusader by nature, and cabinet committees can do without crusaders. Frank could never have made himself completely impartial.

It's not that he'd have wanted to preach, but he'd have had preconceived notions about most of the subjects under discussion.

In self-defence, I must express doubt as to whether any Labour Leader of the Lords would have cut much ice in a cabinet where my only cabinet colleague was the Lord Chancellor, Gerald Gardiner, a noble idealist, outside party politics. It may be that if I had spent years in the Commons with other cabinet members it would have been different. As it was, I was really an outsider.

I was left with plenty of time to spare for the House of Lords itself, and took enormous trouble to be helpful to individuals of all parties. My secretaries seem to have been loyal to me in what they said on that subject to my biographer Mary Craig.

I was handicapped at critical moments by not having any departmental assistance, although I had some outstanding private secretaries. As well as Angela Lambert there were Douglas Tanner, Thelma Cross and Barbara Brierley. Michael Wheeler-Booth, now distinguished Clerk of Parliament, serviced the Chief Whip, Malcolm Shepherd, later an effective Leader of the House and myself; a quizzical smile was never far from his face.

In 1966, the crucial issue arose as to whether to devalue or not. I called on the Chancellor of the Exchequer, James Callaghan, and Douglas Jay, President of the Board of Trade, who advised against it. I duly followed that guidance, only to be rebuked by Tony Crosland as the only intellectual against devaluation, which was strongly favoured by himself, Roy Jenkins and Dick Crossman. I was probably wrong in the line I took, and have always retained much sympathy with those who take the wrong option in regard to devaluation.

Many social reforms were introduced during these years. I will mention only those connected with the Home Office. The committee into the causes of crime referred to in the last chapter, entitled *Crime: A Challenge*, over which I presided, bore plenty of fruit. Above all, capital punishment was abolished for all practical purposes. In the last half-century, that is by far the greatest of penal improvements. Parole was introduced, as were other desirable improvements.

Penal reform apart, I was in favour of one of the main liberal reforms, and against another one. In 1956, I had been the
first member of either House to espouse the Wolfenden
Report which proposed the legalisation of homosexual acts
between consenting adults in private. I was referred to at that
time by Bob Boothby as the 'non-playing captain of the homosexual team'. I was happy to think – I am still happy to think –
that the measure was passed into law by our government.
Today, however, my standing with the gay community is not of
the highest, as I have never favoured reducing the age of consent below twenty-one.

Abortion was a very different matter. Technically, the 1967
Bill which became an Act was a Private Member's Bill, introduced by David Steel, but Roy Jenkins, the Home Secretary,
made no secret of his support. The government promised sufficient time which made all the difference. Moreover the Bill
itself was favoured by the great majority of the cabinet. When
it reached the Lords, I took the step, possibly unprecedented,
of leaving my place on the front bench and speaking against
the Bill from the back benches. I admitted even then that
there were some circumstances in which I would agree to abortion in my own family, but I forecast that, whatever the
sponsors said, it would lead to abortion on demand.

This forecast was borne out for me a year later, by which
time I had resigned from the government and started the New
Horizon youth centre in Soho. A young, well-favoured woman
came in and asked me how she could obtain an abortion. I
asked her why she wanted one. She said she wanted to go to
Austria for winter sports with her boyfriend. I said that she
must consult her general physician. She seemed surprised.
She had been told that you only had to ask for one to get one.
It would be untrue to say that abortion is now available on
demand in Britain, but it is much more freely on demand
than we were assured at that time it would be.

The time came, in 1967, when sterling was at last devalued,
and a policy of 'cuts' was embarked on. We were told that
there were to be no sacred cows. One such cut involved the
postponement, an indefinite postponement it seemed at the
time, of the raising of the school-leaving age, which was an

integral part of Labour Party policy and had been promised a few months before. There was a close division in the cabinet. The voting was 11–9 in favour of a postponement. George Brown and Jim Callaghan, who had both left school prematurely, were against it. George Brown, the Deputy Prime Minister, passed my chair as he went out and whispered, 'I think I will go out with you on this one.' He was on his way to a function at the Russian embassy; after that he had to embark on a world tour, and in the event I resigned alone. George later expressed regret that he had not chosen this issue for his resignation, instead of the rather hazy one on which he went out eventually.

My only House of Lords colleague, Gerald Gardiner, made a touching effort to get me to change my mind. He called at my flat and, with all his forensic skill, put the question, 'If you could be genuinely convinced that the school-leaving age was going to be raised within two years, would you reconsider?' By that time it was too late for me to retreat. Ted Short and Tony Greenwood also urged me not to resign. When I did, Gerald Gardiner and my successor, Eddie Shackleton, spoke generously about me in the Lords; but otherwise there was, for a time, a wall of silence between me and my late colleagues. Six months later, I ran into Roy Jenkins who told me, 'I nearly wrote to you at the time.' I replied, I hope not too bitterly, 'I believe a great many colleagues nearly wrote to me at the time.'

Roy's sense of humour is one of his most attractive qualities. He made an excellent story out of the episode in a generous essay he wrote about Elizabeth and me. He tells the story, more or less as I have told it above; he adds that I twice wrote to apologise for any discourtesy. Then comes his punch line, referring to myself: 'He told the story again a few months later.'

Throughout the events leading up to my resignation, and during the resignation itself, no one could have been kinder than Harold Wilson. When I had already indicated my determination to resign, he came to the reception given for Rachel on her wedding day, and spoke appropriately. I introduced him when he arrived to my former secretary, an elderly lady, by that time blind, called Ruth Mottram. When he came to leave, he insisted on saying goodbye to Mrs Mottram; there were no votes in such a gesture, just human kindliness.

I am bound to say that when I finally took my leave he was not so much concerned with my departure as with the possibility that Jenny Lee, widow of Aneurin Bevan, might resign over the Health Service charges. I have long held the opinion that, generally speaking, when a cabinet minister resigns, the position has been reached where the PM is happy to see him go (there has not yet been a female resignation from a cabinet). This may well have been the case on this occasion. If so, Harold Wilson concealed it gracefully. In later years we became genuine friends in the Lords, before and after illness overtook him.

A few general words about Harold Wilson seem appropriate. As well as his kindness, which is now widely acknowledged, I must not fail to mention his sheer intelligence. I have said somewhere in a book review that he was the only prime minister since Asquith who had a first-class degree from Oxford. It was pointed out to me that Anthony Eden had a first in oriental languages, but when I was a don at Christ Church, Eden's college, this was never referred to – for whatever reason. Wilson had a dazzling first in Philosophy, Politics and Economics. He was also, at his best, an exceptionally witty speaker.

No student of the time should fail to read the splendid life of Harold Wilson by Ben Pimlott (1992) and, no doubt, Philip Ziegler's official biography (unpublished as I write) will be absolutely first class. Pimlott brings out very clearly Wilson's determination to remain a provincial and not to enter the metropolitan Establishment. This was so deep a part of his character that it is no good wishing that it had been otherwise. But, in the event, the Establishment, whether Conservative, Labour (Gaitskellite) or official, regarded him with a certain reservation throughout his career. He was forced by circumstances into a left-wing position, but was never really a man of the Left. He must be given credit for winning four out of five elections and holding the party together for thirteen years. He was much criticised for his choice of friends and nomination of peers, but as one who helped to introduce two of the latter into the Lords, and as a friend of Marcia Williams and Joe Kagan, I would never cast a stone against him on that ground.

I have already mentioned the Two-Writ plan, brainchild of Henry Burrows, Assistant Clerk in the Lords, under which hereditary peers would be allowed to speak in the House, but not to vote. You may remember that Henry and I nearly fell out over his untimely enthusiasm for the scheme on the seventh green.

When I became the Leader of the House, Henry, alas, had been denied the top position he had been entitled to, had left the service of the Lords, and had moved away from the neighbourhood. But there was a moment when his great idea seemed to be about to come out of retirement. When I first proposed the scheme to the cabinet it was not taken seriously, as Dick Crossman records in his *Diaries*. When, however, Dick became Leader of the Commons, the picture changed and he became its most effective advocate. It was accepted by the Leaders of the government and the opposition in the Commons and Lords. Eventually, however, I resigned from the cabinet and Dick was moved to another ministry. In the Commons a distinguished but, in my view, unholy alliance of Michael Foot, left-wing Labour, and Enoch Powell, right-wing Conservative, persuaded their colleagues that this Bill would strengthen the Lords at the expense of the Commons. Sadly the proposal is not likely to reappear in the future.

17
HUMILITY

Throughout 1968 I was engaged in the production of a small book, *Humility*, published in 1969. Reading it again I am struck by my obsessive concern to relate humility to a career in the world. Many years later, I wrote a book called *Suffering*, whose title the publishers expanded very sensibly into *Suffering and Hope*. My book on humility might well have been titled 'Humility and Ambition'. I am amused to notice what was said about humility by some great figures of the time. Lord Thomson of Fleet, owner of *The Times* among other papers, commented, when he heard I was writing a book on humility, 'Humility – I've got no use for it. Where would I be if I had been humble?' Later he added, 'I'll tell you why I'm so much against humility, Frank. It's because humility is utterly opposed to salesmanship.'

Mary Wilson, wife of the Prime Minister at that time, told me, 'I should like to see the book, but I'm no good on humility at the moment.' Her eyes flashed as she said it. A gentle personality breathed fire. She added, 'My mother used to teach me to turn the other cheek, but the point came when righteous indignation was justified.' 'You mean', I put in, 'on behalf of someone else?' 'Yes,' she said. 'Harold always tells me that I am like a lioness in defence of my cubs.' She left me in no doubt that her husband, maltreated by the press, was one of the cubs.

My great friend and best man, the late Freddie Birkenhead, put a point of view that I found widespread when I told him that I was looking for men with humility who had succeeded in politics. 'It is rather a contradiction in terms,' he told me gently.

Lord Beaverbrook put the same point in another way, while recognising the scriptural instruction to do justice and to love mercy and to walk humbly. 'The quality of humility', he said to me, 'is by far the most difficult to attain. There is something deep down in the successful man of affairs which seems to conflict with it. His career is imbued with a sense of struggle and courage and conquest and seems almost to invite arrogance.' I could not disguise from myself in 1968 that I had embarked on politics in the Conservative Research Department thirty-eight years before with a fair share of ambition, and had been animated during the years that followed by the same spark.

Among outstanding men of my acquaintance I selected Lord Attlee, Lord Alexander of Tunis, President de Valera and Lord Halifax as notably humble. I could never forget Attlee diffidently asking me to pay the restaurant with my cheque, which he would repay, because 'They don't know me here.' Field Marshal Lord Alexander, I had been told, used to make morning tea for his batman when he was sick. De Valera, whose biography I helped to write, convinced me that he would have preferred to spend his life in teaching. Halifax could undoubtedly have been Prime Minister in 1940 if he had lifted a finger but he considered, rightly, that Churchill would make a better war leader.

I still feel today that anyone who is seriously interested in the concept of humility would benefit from reading my little book. I could point out that, at the time, with the exception of Bishop Ullathorne in the last century, no one had written a book about humility. Bishop Ullathorne, when asked if there was any good book on the subject, mentioned his own. But his book was not remembered in 1969, and, I am afraid, still less remembered now. It seems that humility (like, it might be thought, ambition) is too elusive a subject for the finest brains to deal with systematically, although it is referred to in a thousand books, spiritual and otherwise. If I were writing that book now I would want to say more about self-esteem. Self-esteem is the fashionable word in social work today, but none the worse for that.

A little while ago I visited Streetwise, an impressive centre for young male prostitutes. They pride themselves, justifiably I think, on raising the self-esteem of their young visitors. In one of their brochures a young visitor pays tribute to the work of the centre: 'I'm not proud of being a male prostitute, but now I am proud of being me.' They have since closed down.

Not long ago I opened an exhibition of prisoners' art. The dedicated art teacher asked me to say something about the effect of prisoners' artistic creations in raising their self-esteem. 'Their self-esteem', she told me, 'is pitiably low, but it is greatly improved when they paint a picture and somebody says that it's quite good.'

Few of us, I think, would preach humility to outcasts and those who have fallen by the wayside.

The crucial pages of the book for me now are those which summarise what I call the Teaching of Christ. I still like the assertion that 'Christianity begins with Christ and in a sense ends there'. I cannot refrain from quoting once again the never-to-be-forgotten sentence from John's Gospel: 'Rising from supper he laid his garments aside and began to wash the feet of the disciples.'

I still find the analysis in my final chapter very helpful. 'Humility', I wrote, 'involves these ideas at least:

i   knowledge of oneself as one is

ii   the opposite of pride

iii   meekness in conduct

iv   obedience

v   service

I can only speak of my own practice. For years I prayed for more humility, but now I couple that prayer with one for more self-esteem. If that little book were ever re-published, self-esteem would require an honoured place.

18
ACTIVE RETIREMENT
1968–93

Since 1968, the House of Lords has played a large part in my life. My forty-eight years of membership do not compare with Billy Listowel's service of sixty-two years but they are bound to promote a few reflections.

I have told earlier the story of Bobbety, Marquess of Salisbury, reassuring a Labour critic with the words, 'You were quite right to say what you felt it was your duty to say. This is a House of Parliament, not a club.' But in fact, in the eyes of many of us, the Lords is the best club in the world; a state of affairs to which Bobbety Salisbury made a unique contribution. From the very beginning he was determined to welcome the small herd of Labour members and make them feel thoroughly at home. Today as we sit together at the 'long table' when we do not have guests, there is no obvious division of party or class. The House of Lords is the least snobbish place in the world. When an illustrious duke paid one of his rare visits, it was pointed out that he had not taken his seat in the current session and he was temporarily removed from the Chamber.

I have long thought that the House of Lords has the best debates and the worst voting system in the world. In the debates on social questions, I am impressed again and again by the heartfelt and very expert contributions by noble Lords and Ladies who have given years to these matters. Baroness Faithfull, now (if she allows me to say so) in her eighties,

speaks with special authority as a former director of Social
Services in Oxford – the only professional social worker in the
House. She sits on the Conservative benches and (described
by me as the 'mole of compassion') fires many a broadside at
the relevant minister.

Everyone visiting the Lords is struck by the outstanding
courtesy of the debates. No one who adopts a tone of personal hostility to a minister or backbencher gets away with it.
It is possible to look at this extreme courtesy from another
angle. A gifted writer in the *Guardian* in July 1993 set out to
'send up' the whole thing with reference to Noble Lords and
Noble Baronesses and Lordships and Ladyships and all the
rest of it.

Soon after I came to the Lords, some tough shop stewards
from the Clyde came visiting me. I asked what they thought of
the ceremonial. They said, and a Labour government was in
power at the time, 'It's all right so long as it's on our side.' In
party terms that could not be said to have been true of the
Lords at any time. But if the *Guardian* journalist had listened
to one of the debates on social questions, she would have had
a good deal to think about.

Over the years the atmosphere has altered very little,
although the number of participants is at least double what it
was when I arrived. The most striking change has been the
coming of the women; the first four among the first life peers
in 1958. Someone who admires and knows the House better
than anyone has referred to it in my hearing as a 'heterosexual
place'. That would not be true of debates on defence or economics, but on social matters the voice of the women is
sometimes dominant.

For a long time their coming was resisted – for forty years, in
fact, after they were allowed the vote in the Commons. The
resistance was led by a bearded admiral, who voiced a widespread if ludicrous question as to what would happen in
regard to the lavatories. Of course, a deeper prejudice lay concealed. One of the four ladies to be ennobled was Baroness
Ravensdale, daughter of the Marquess Curzon of Kedleston. I
said to the admiral who had headed the opposition, 'Don't you
think Irene is doing a good job?' He replied very seriously,

'When I see that long neck bending over, I wish I had my chopper and I would go chop, chop, chop.'

One of the first four women introduced was my dear, much-admired friend Barbara (Baroness) Wootton, economist and criminologist, whom I had the honour of sponsoring. She, a leading humanist, was one of the first peers to ask for the alternative form of words instead of taking the oath. I shall never forget standing at the Clerk's table while they hunted for the missing wording. As her senior sponsor, I stood opposite the bench of the Conservative ex-ministers. They became very restive as the search continued. One old fellow whose name escapes me, hard of hearing, said in a very loud voice to Lord Swinton beside him, 'What's the trouble, Philip?' Swinton, speaking very loudly to make himself heard, replied, 'She doesn't believe in God.' The hard-of-hearing peer, speaking more loudly still, pressed the question, 'Why the devil not, Philip?' Swinton, a man full of his own kind of humour replied, 'You'd better ask her.' By this time, the missing words had been discovered.

More than twenty years later I helped to introduce Mary (Baroness) Warnock, like Barbara a real intellectual's intellectual. I had several times been hospitably received by Mary and her husband Geoffrey, Principal of Hertford College, Oxford and later Vice-Chancellor, when I preached at Hertford. Since then Mary has been a distinguished Principal of Girton and headed more than one important government committee. We have not seen eye-to-eye on embryos, but she is one of many who give the House of Lords a good name.

Women peers (Barbara Wootton taught me never to refer to them as peeresses) have occupied many key positions in the Lords in recent times, always to general satisfaction. Janet Young was Leader of the House, Pat Llewellyn-Davies was government Chief Whip, Bea Serota and Eirene White deputy chairmen of committees. On the government front bench at the time of writing are four formidable ladies. Baroness Chalker, I would argue, has the best elocution in the House. At the end of the Maastricht debate it was impossible to find a seat, and I had to listen to Linda Chalker through a crowd standing at the bar. I could hear every word perfectly. Emily

139

Blatch handled the endless debates on the Education Bill with extraordinary resilience.

When I joined the House in 1945 I was (this is not a boast) the fastest speaker in the estimation of the *Hansard* staff. Arnold Goodman, arguably the most entertaining speaker in recent years, left me trailing. I asked one of the *Hansard* staff what he'd got that I hadn't. They had no doubt about the answer: 'He never pauses between paragraphs.' Looking at Arnold's massive chest I saw that he had an advantage there, but Emily Blatch is faster still and her mind moves as quickly as her words. She is said to be part of the East Anglia Mafia; in other words, very close to John Major. I hope that he remains Prime Minister long enough to put her in the cabinet.

Julia Cumberlege is a genuine expert on the administration of mental health and special hospitals. I refrain from paying her any more compliments because of those she has paid to me on my book, *Prisoner or Patient.* Baroness Denton is that rare phenomenon in the House of Lords, a successful businesswoman. But so, among crossbenchers, is Detta O'Cathain, director of the Barbican, but maintaining at all times, not in name only, the honour of Ireland.

On the Labour benches we have recently received some new stars. Baroness Hollis, Patricia, former leader of the Norwich City Council and lecturer at the University of East Anglia, is one of the four glamour girls that have recently enriched the Labour group in the Lords. One of the others is Tessa Blackstone, Master (a strange title for a supreme feminist) of Birkbeck College. I asked a leading Conservative peer what he thought of one of her speeches. He replied, 'I never listen to what she says, I just look at her.' Another of these striking ladies is Ann Mallalieu, the first woman to become President of the Cambridge Union. Still under fifty, she is a QC and Recorder. Finally there is Margaret Jay, daughter of ex-Prime Minister Callaghan, who presided at one time over the British embassy in Washington when her husband, Peter Jay, was ambassador. His father was Douglas Jay, at one time President of the Board of Trade. None of these ladies appears to like extravagant compliments, but they can't prevent them being paid behind their backs. On one occasion while Patricia

Hollis was speaking, a colleague admiring her long, slim figure turned to me and described her as 'a well-tuned filly'.

These and others in the House who are just or just under fifty introduce an amount of mental liveliness to go with their physical charms. I hasten to say that my close affinities remain with their older sisters, though none of these is in my age bracket. Not long before writing I opened debates initiated in highly expert fashion by Nora David on adult education and Doris Fisher on local government services. Lena Jaeger has been chair of the Labour Party, Wendy Nichol a one-time deputy chief whip. Women such as these come into public life after raising families and serving usually in local government. Many women who enter the Commons are similarly equipped; what of Elizabeth's niece, Harriet Harman, for whom great things are rightly prophesied?

It seems that a Labour government would be committed to excluding hereditary peers from the Lords, though no one can say whether they would make the attempt in the first parliament, possibly with a small majority. For myself, biased as I may be, the whole idea of an elected House is distasteful. I feel sure we would finish up with a second-rate personnel compared to what we possess at present.

No other chamber in the world possesses our unique collection of eminent ecclesiastics, jurists, leading academics, business chiefs, ex-trades union leaders and government servants of the highest distinction. In the last resort, it is true that the Conservatives can whip up a majority, but the quality of the preceding debates is surely unequalled in the world.

If peers are to be appointed, then I would agree with those who say that it should not be left entirely to the personal choice of the prime minister. Some representative commission should be set up to play a crucial part in the selection.

It should be understood that my innumerable speeches in the Lords have usually been based on personal experience, whether prison visiting, which I have been involved in since the thirties, the anti-pornography campaign which I became notoriously associated with in 1971, publishing (I was chairman of Sidgwick & Jackson from 1981 to 1985), or various social concerns. The latter have included helping to found the New Horizon youth centre in 1968, and carrying the 'Alf Morris Bill' to assist the handicapped through the Lords in 1970, as well as special initiatives in recent years, one concerned with hospices for the dying, the other with the new universities.

My connection with youth work goes back a long way. It began when I was an adolescent, no older than the older boys of the Eton Manor boys' club in Hackney Wick, East London. The presiding genius of the club was my mother's brother, Arthur Villiers, DSO, merchant banker, athlete, soldier, philanthropist, freeman of Leyton, freeman of Hackney Wick, who lived at or near the club for half a century.

I loved all vigorous games, the vigour declining as the years increased. I ran races, played netball or basketball, tennis, squash and rugger. I played for the Eton Manor rugby fifteen in their inaugural match, getting my eye cut open. I was never much good at billiards, but there was a time when at table tennis I could compete with all except the London champions. I played quite a bit of squash with Douglas Jardine, who showed me scant mercy.

Many years later I initiated the first debate ever held on the youth service in the Lords. While still in the Wilson cabinet I persuaded Harold Wilson to allow me to undertake an inquiry into the problems of youth. When I resigned, my first instinct was to set up some kind of establishment devoted to the problems of young delinquents. Even before I got going in that direction I played, for a time, a central part in the student revolution, in the sense of becoming chairman of the Hornsey Commission, set up jointly by staff and students (more enthusiastically by the latter than by the former) to lay plans for a happier future for the Hornsey College of Art.

I well remember the jovial address of the chairman of governors, a man prominent in the laundry business. 'I know you fellows,' cried the Alderman to the students, 'you think I don't know about academic life. You're quite right, I don't. But I know what it is like having to wash your shirts and I can tell you it is a very nasty job.' The student revolution passed and, with valuable help, I started the New Horizon youth centre. I was quickly dissuaded from the idea of confining it to delinquents.

It was and has remained open to anybody but more particularly to the homeless.

When we started it was indeed in a small way. Our office was so small that Nikki Hunt, the charismatic secretary and my dear friend from that day to this, and I could not be accommodated at the same time. One of us had to work in the passage. We were joined by Martin Walker, a leader in the Hornsey 'revolution', also charismatic but hostile to the Establishment in a manner that was not mine. Others came in to help us who deserve mention; most particularly Jon Snow (whom I mentioned previously), who has gone on to greatness but has retained his interest in New Horizon, of which he is chairman today.

We moved into slightly better premises, and have now been in Macklin Street, Soho, for many years. In the early days I shared a lavatory with drug addicts who used it for the purpose of 'fixing'. Jon has told me that of the three hundred drug addicts who used the centre at the beginning of 1972, twenty were dead by the end of the year. There came a time when drug addicts were accommodated elsewhere.

New Horizon, of which I am today a patron, has gone from strength to strength. Today there are twelve social workers, and something like 3,000 young people are seen in the centre every year and assisted with every aspect of their lives. The need of the homeless young, however, is more acute than ever. The government bears a heavy responsibility, although it is no good pretending that all responsibility is theirs.

In the summer of 1970, I was greatly privileged to be asked to take through the Lords the Bill for the disabled which should always be associated with its creator, Alf Morris, MP, later the first Minister for the Disabled. I had not been involved with the disabled before, except in the sense that for some years before I went into the Wilson government, I was chairman of the National Society for the Mentally Handicapped, now Mencap, gloriously represented in the House of Lords by its former chairman, David, Lord Renton, and the driving force behind its progress in recent years, Brian, Lord Rix, both of whom are parents of severely handicapped children.

I hope and believe that those who love handicapped children will forgive one amusing recollection. Harry (Lord) Nathan took me to visit the famous Jewish Home for the Handicapped – Ravenswood. One boy prodded Harry in his ample stomach, asking 'Fat, fat, why are you fat?' I laughed heartily till he switched to me, patted me on the bald part of my head which I bent down to him, and asked 'Bald, bald, why are you bald?' Then it was Harry's turn to laugh heartily.

In introducing the second reading of the Disabled Bill, I used a phrase which I have no wish to improve on. 'Suffering', I said, 'while it often degrades, can sometimes ennoble.' It was not difficult to perceive illustrations of the latter proposition on the floor of the House in 1970. Sue Masham, Davina d'Arcy de Knayth, Mike Crawshaw and Martin Ingleby, all crippled for life, all speaking from wheelchairs, were an inspiring phenomenon. Here, certainly, no other legislature in the world could rival us. Since then they have been joined by others also afflicted. I stand back in awe in the face of their unfailing cheerfulness.

But they would be the first to point out that they have been granted the opportunity to bring their disability to public attention in a fashion denied to the disabled generally. I have come to know well the quiet heroism in the face of suffering which is exhibited by countless ordinary people; the sufferers and those who care for them.

The year 1970 was an important one for me in other ways too. It was the year in which I first met my dear friend and colleague Gwen Keeble, and in which I took up the reins of a new career as a publisher.

Gwen has been deeply involved in all my activities ever since. She worked full time with me when I was chairman of Sidgwick & Jackson, although she had already retired after a successful career in banking, industry and the civil service spanning forty-eight years.

Gwen Keeble is by common consent a phenomenon. At seventeen, she won a scholarship to university, but family circumstances made it more expedient for her to train for a business career. She is widely read, an accomplished linguist, having spent a year at Bonn as a mature student, subsequently being seconded to Berlin on an assignment brought to a sudden close by the outbreak of war. When I was writing my books on Saint Francis of Assisi and President Kennedy, the chapters on Saint Clare and Jackie Kennedy were really hers.

Till recently, just turned ninety (though looking twenty-five years younger), she came up once a week from Hove, walking from Victoria Station to the House of Lords carrying a heavy bag. Slim, elegantly dressed, with her silvery-grey hair and stylish glasses, she has made a significant impression on the many who have come to know her in the Lords.

It was entirely due to the kindness of Charles (now Lord) Forte that I became chairman of Sidgwick & Jackson, a small publishing house with an honourable record. In January 1971 Charles was prompted in that direction by my son-in-law Hugh Fraser, whose innumerable friends are still lamenting his premature death. Charles is a devout Catholic and may have been prejudiced in my favour on that account. For the next fifteen years I worked at number 42 Museum Street (I still think of it as the ideal location for a publisher), ten as chairman, five as a director.

At the same time I was involved in numerous other activities, most notably in pornography in 1971 to 1972. I was therefore in one sense, but not in another, a hands-on chairman. I was paid a part-time salary but I attended the office every day.

The atmosphere was delightful throughout, entirely due to the rare personality of William Armstrong, managing director. If William had been more ambitious he would be known as a great publisher. As it is he is respected by all and thought of by all who worked with him with gratitude. The mention of great publishers reminds me that I was at one point selected as one of the five great publishers of the year. I should never have accepted the honour, which should have gone to William.

Margaret Willes, literary editor for ten years, supplied a distinguished presence and a wide culture. Stephen du Sautoy, son of the chairman of Faber, today a very successful bookseller, was so brilliant a publicity chief that, though quite small, we won the prize for best publicity performance three years running. Bill Procter, our production manager, possessed a deep love of books which, I suppose in my ignorance, I had hardly expected to find in a working printer. Nigel Newton, our sales director, had a sure instinct for the number of copies that a book would sell; but even more attractive in my eyes was his literary intuition, deriving partly at least from his Cambridge degree in English literature. He used to insist that we would never be a great publisher until we published a good quantity of quality literature. I supported him too weakly on this. He has since made a great success of Bloomsbury Publishing.

We were handicapped from first to last by the need to make reasonable profits immediately. We were inhibited, or thought we were, from taking a long view. My friend George Weidenfeld, whom incidentally I had the honour of helping to introduce to the House of Lords, has rendered many services to my family, not least his readiness to allow them to take a long time over their books. Elizabeth spent eight years writing her two-volume *Life of Wellington*. Antonia has always been given ample time to write her bestselling biographies, beginning with *Mary Queen of Scots*. Thomas took ten years over his *Boer War*, and more than ten over his *Scramble for Africa*, which won the W.H. Smith prize for the book of the year. We at Sidgwick were engaged, or thought we were engaged, in a scramble for survival. We used to expect our authors to produce their books in a year or not much more.

William Armstrong, in a short account of Sidgwick & Jackson, has picked out General Hackett's book *The Third World War*, which sold three million copies, as our most successful venture. The book he was proudest to publish was *Live Aid: The Greatest Show on Earth*, which raised over £1 million for the relief of the Ethiopian famine in 1985; this led to *Is That It?* (1986), the autobiography of Live Aid founder Bob Geldof (700,000 copies sold in the UK and Commonwealth).

Most of the best suggestions for books came from William or Margaret, but I can at least claim that it was I who wrote on behalf of the firm to invite Ted Heath to write *Sailing*. This became a bestseller, as did his books on music and travel. Even now, however, credit for the idea is hotly disputed in the firm.

I obtained particular pleasure from publishing Diana Mosley's life of the Duchess of Windsor, and John Grigg's life of Nancy Astor – cases where what William has called my 'contacts' came in useful.

As I said, Sidgwick was a small firm when I joined, but in three years we had quadrupled, and since then the firm has gone from strength to strength – though I still think that Museum Street was a more romantic place for publishers than Fulham, where the office is now.

If I say that I loved the life of publishing I am not exaggerating, but, I must be honest, part of the joy existed in the lunches at the Garrick and the Gay Hussar. It was in the latter restaurant that I entertained Diana and Oswald Mosley after we had published Diana's finely written book about the Duchess of Windsor. At the next table were Michael Foot and a friend. Michael Foot was a particular star in the New Horizon and, one assumed, a particular enemy of all that Tom Mosley had ever stood for. However, when he left the restaurant he came across and said beamingly 'What a pleasure to see you here, Sir Oswald.' Tom Mosley, when Michael left, kept repeating, 'How like England; it could only happen in England.'

The Garrick has always had glamour for me – before I was elected in 1971, while I was a member, and in the years since I resigned. When I left publishing, I could not justify belonging to a club I never used. It had awkward standards of its own, at any rate when I joined. During my early days as a member, I took to lunch a well-known literary agent. A senior member who had promoted my election took me aside next day. 'I warn you,' he said, 'you made a good start here, but if you don't mind my saying so, it would be wiser for you not to ask any more literary agents.' 'Can't I', I asked deferentially, 'invite Graham Watson, my own literary agent, universally esteemed?' The senior member stroked his chin. 'Well, well,' he agreed, 'I might possibly make a concession for Graham.'

One thing I cannot understand about the Garrick is their persistent refusal to admit women. But then I am an uncomprehending feminist. Not that everything the feminists say or do is sensible – on abortion, of course, but on many other things beside abortion. Nevertheless I shall go to my grave demanding equality of the sexes.

1971 brought me much notoriety, welcome or unwelcome, but also a single honour. In March of that year I received a letter from Michael Adeane, the Queen's private secretary, inviting me to become a Knight of the Garter. It would be an understatement to say I was delighted. Dickie Mountbatten described it as an 'imaginative appointment', which was another way of saying that it surprised him as it surprised me. Harold Wilson put it in a different perspective when talking to Mary Craig: 'No one was a more likely candidate at that time. There were vacancies, and the Queen needed a retired Labour minister for one of them. Frank had been a minister of cabinet rank as far back as her father's reign; he was undoubtedly the most obvious choice.'

There are, by custom, twenty-four non-royal Knights of the most Noble Order of the Garter, founded in 1348 by Edward III. At the time of writing (March 1993) the composition (there is one vacancy) is something like this: ten 'big wigs' – lord lieutenants or such like; seven politicians; three Service chiefs and three others, a former Governor of the Bank of England, Lord Hunt of Everest and Lord Sainsbury, a mighty philanthropist. Of the politicians – or 'elder statesmen' – four are Labour; the former Prime Ministers, Wilson and Callaghan, and the former Leaders of the Lords, Shackleton and myself. The Conservatives are Heath, Hailsham and Lord Carrington, former Home Secretary. The Queen has been notably careful to make sure that Labour politicians have their full share of the knighthoods; a good example of her determined impartiality between the parties.

Elizabeth has been involved for many years with many aspects of royalty, historical and contemporary. Before a large audience at Hay-on-Wye her views on the future of the monarchy were opposed by Roy Hattersley, at the time recently retired as Deputy Leader of the Labour Party. I look upon him as the only politician since Disraeli who has written high-class novels. He concentrated his attack on the monarchy as promoting an unhealthy deference throughout the nation. In the course of his remarks he singled out Mary Robinson, the glamorous President of Ireland, as the right kind of head of state. I told him of my recent meeting with Mrs Robinson, whom I had met and admired in academic circles in the past.

I was one of the reception line at the Irish Centre of which I am president, when she paid a visit. When she came to me, she said, 'We have met before, several times.' I bowed my head. She said, 'I understand you have done good work for this centre?' I bowed again. She said 'Have you lost your voice?' I said 'Respect,' and bowed for the third time.

I asked Hattersley what he would do when confronted with royalty or, for that matter, a republican head of state. He thought for a moment, then said, roguishly, 'I would incline my head.' On the whole I think that I rather over-do the deference. Year after year the Queen and other members of the royal family pass along the line of Garter Knights and their wives before lunch. I never say a word; Elizabeth speaks up more boldly and, I now think, more helpfully. I am considering a braver style of address next year.

I am proud to have been the first to press on the House of Lords two vital causes: the hospices for the dying, and the polytechnics. In each case others, like Caroline (Baroness) Cox, had been at work for many years before I came into the field. When I was preparing my book on suffering I visited four hospices and benefited far more than the hospices did from the visits.

A few extracts from the noble personalities in charge should convey a little of the flavour. A hospice, I was told by a doctor at St Joseph's, Hackney, usually regarded as the first hospice established in Britain, told me, is a caring community whose purpose is to look after those for whom cure is no longer appropriate. In popular parlance, a hospice is usually a place for the dying, and St Joseph's was described in just that way on its iron gates for many years. Now the public emphasis is much more on life than death.

I am much honoured to be a patron of St Michael's, Hastings, which I suppose I can regard as my local hospice. I was told by a young woman doctor that at the end of each day she said to God: 'Well, I have done my best for today. I leave the rest to you.' The great Dame Cecily Saunders of St Christopher's repeated the emphasis of the doctor at St Joseph's. 'The hospice is about living until you die, no matter how long it takes. Trust and faith in living and trust and faith in dying. People come with awe and fear towards death, and we hope that by staying with them and helping them to trust each day that they are living, they will trust in the next step and be able to see Jesus in a new way.' But she insists this spiritual movement may not be expressed in woes, and that at all times, 'People have to make their own journey.'

Dr Sheila Cassidy, now medical director of a hospice in Plymouth, who achieved world fame when she was imprisoned in Chile, has coined what to me is perhaps the most inspiring of all the relevant mottos: 'Sharing the darkness'. She took me to see two patients in her hospice, where the average stay before the end comes is about three weeks. One had a large part of her face eaten away by cancer. Another was a young woman of twenty-seven with a child of fifteen months. They assured me that the life of the hospice was 'magnificent'. Sheila told me, 'We must enter into the suffering of the dying patients and in some way share their pain.' It was a rare privilege for me to be allowed to discuss these matters with people like her.

Since I first raised the matter in the Lords, the government has been somewhat more forthcoming in its assistance to the hospices. But far, far more ought to be done to help them carry out ever more effectively their humanitarian and spiritual work.

With the polytechnics it has been what I can only call a success story. I have been associated in many minds with losing causes. '*Victrix causa deis placuit, sed victa Catoni*' has been said of me, by no means unkindly. But in the case of the polytechnics the wall of Jericho fell almost overnight. The binary system which, I have to admit, I defended as a government spokesman many years earlier, resulted in the polytechnics being by definition inferior to the universities and those who attended them second-class students. But I was able to argue, with support from those more expert than myself, that the academic standards in the polys were just as good as those in many universities. I proclaimed in the Lords with some passion that the binary system must go, and sure enough it went. It would be ludicrous to give myself too heavy a pat on the back for the result, but I cherish the secret thought that I made a distinct difference. I was delighted that when I was made an honorary fellow of the new University of Westminster, my companion in receipt of the honour was Caroline Cox, who had laboured in and for the polytechnics for many years. We received our fellowships, appropriately, from the hands of Sara Hogg, *éminence grise* of the Prime Minister and daughter-in-law of Quintin Hogg, whose family will always be associated with the rise of the Polytechnic of Central London, now this same University of Westminster.

When I ceased to be any kind of publisher on reaching the age of eighty, I was joined in a charitable effort, designated HELP, by Jenny Mackilligin – a fine-looking young woman who has worked for me ever since without remuneration. She pays regular visits to special hospital and prisons, reads to the blind and does voluntary work for MIND. I am indeed fortunate.

19
PORNOGRAPHY

In the late spring of 1971, I opened a debate in the Lords on pornography. I boldly announced: 'Pornography has increased, is increasing and ought to be diminished.' I received something like 5,000 letters approving of the stand I was taking, many of them from evangelical sources. There was plenty of ridicule to come. Soon after the debate I set up a large and extremely distinguished committee. We produced a voluminous report eighteen months later.

I have certain qualifications, and certain disqualifications, for discussing this subject. On the one hand, I have so much distaste for pornography that I am not open to the criticism that there is something prurient in my concern with it. The word prurient was once used about me in this connection. It led to the only threat of legal action that I have ever issued. The writer, a well-known journalist, apologised the next week and explained that he had looked up the word and found that it meant something different from what he imagined. On the other hand this same distaste for dirty films, sleazy bookshops and sex shows has prevented me from becoming a long-term expert. Mary Whitehouse, feeling equal distaste but made of sterner stuff, initiated the struggle against pornography seven years before I touched it and has continued to denounce it to the present day. She has created the National Viewers' and Listeners' Association, which has 165,000 members – an amazing feat.

What an extraordinary career hers has been. In her early fifties she was a teacher of art and sex education (highly relevant as it proved). Thirty years later she is accepted all over the world as the supreme opponent of pornography and champion of moral purity. As I write these lines I have been to the launch for her new book *Quite Contrary*. She arrived rather late, having been besieged by press interviewers in flattering fashion. Yesterday I was recommending the book to the Prime Minister to see if he is really concerned with traditional moral values. I have reviewed it for the *Catholic Herald* suggesting that no living English woman has had a greater influence for good. I have nominated it for *The Tablet* as the best book of the year.

It should be mentioned that at the time of my investigation violence had not become the central issue that it is today. Our report devoted only one chapter to violence. When Mary Whitehouse and I did battle before the Cambridge Union against John Mortimer, now a delightful friend, and a sex doctor, I cannot remember violence being mentioned. It would be very different now.

I have often been asked how I became so interested in pornography. It is often assumed that it has been a lifelong obsession. I am not readily believed if I say that the word never crossed my lips in public until I announced my House of Lords motion for 21 April 1971. By that time, I admit, I had walked out of a play called *America Hurrah* when a huge four-letter word revealed itself before my petrified gaze, and from the musical *O! Calcutta*, though my mind was more than halfway made up against it by the time I went to see it.

Our committee, if over-large, included many notable figures. The Archbishop of Canterbury regretfully told me that he was unsympathetic. He thought that we were calling undue attention to a secondary issue. But the Archbishop of York, Dr Coggan, later Archbishop of Canterbury, joined us on his own initiative. So did one of the leading law lords. So did TV stars like Cliff Richard and Jimmy Savile. So did Kingsley Amis and his then wife Elizabeth Jane Howard, though they attached their own reservations to the report. Most valuable of all, perhaps, was Professor Norman Anderson, equally eminent in

153

legal and theological studies. My great friend Malcolm Muggeridge joined us, partly, I think, as a kindness to me. He detested pornography but he detested government interference, censorship, just as much. He produced a sub-committee report which tried to reconcile his two detestations. A leading feminist, Jill Tweedie, found the same difficulty.

No one could claim that we did not investigate the matter thoroughly, although I was never quite clear as to whether we were an investigatory or campaigning committee.

At the time in intellectual circles – in what would now be called the 'chattering classes' – it was widely reported that Denmark had solved the problems by removing all restrictions on so-called pornography. Therefore, to Denmark it was a duty to go. Led by me, a party of six descended on Copenhagen with almost every national newspaper represented on the aeroplane that carried us there. We had valuable sociological talk. The climax, however, was obviously our visit to two clubs where live sex was to be witnessed. My companion was Dr Christine Saville, who had already been very helpful to me in New Horizon and in later years became the life and soul of the Institute of Study and Treatment of Delinquency. Christine proved more implacably scientific than myself and stayed to the end. I fled from each club in turn.

It must be borne in mind that Christine and I were performing in the eyes of the world press and television. At the first club, a tall, rangy, dynamic figure, apparently, though I believe not actually, female soon emerged brandishing a whip which she offered to anyone wishing to use it on her. Dr Saville surveyed the performer through her horn-rimmed glasses with a frigidity that would have mesmerised a stoat. I goggled nervously through my gold rims. The lady took my measure. She strung the whip round my neck and vibrated me for a few seconds – it seemed like minutes. The next moment she was on my neighbour's lap caressing him indescribably amidst mounting response from the audience. The cameras were all too obviously getting ready for her next move. But my next move was still more obvious to me. At one moment, as seen through the eyes of one newspaper, I was sitting there like a stage professor in a house of ill fame.

The next my seat was empty – I had struck for home.

The publicity, when the report came out, was overwhelming. The report itself was given massive coverage, only the *Guardian* refusing to take it seriously. The more popular *Express, Mail* and *Mirror* were enthusiastic, while *The Times* and the *Telegraph* were more cautious. Hostile reviews appeared in the *New Statesman, Listener* and *Observer*. The anonymous critic in the *TLS* displayed an hysterical contempt. There was consolation to be found in Cyril Connolly's assessment in *The Sunday Times,* and no one represented the literary establishment more obviously than he did. Cyril found the report to be 'respect-worthy, reasonable, well-documented, cool, unbiased and in no sense an inquisition'. One could hardly ask for more.

I myself was made one of the *Daily/Sunday Express* men of the year, along with the winning Olympic equestrian team which included Mark Phillips. In *The Times* it was said that, having been a 'relatively obscure politician', I had become a folk hero. Panorama did a profile on me, in which they filmed me galloping round Tullynally Castle on an Arab steed, with the heroin addicts at New Horizon, investigating the Soho porn shops, and even in church.

Looking back, I feel that this must have been quite embarrassing to other members of the committee. All things considered they showed great tolerance and kindness towards me. An old friend, Basil Rookeley, a valued member of the committee, told me recently that he thought that there was no doubt about the merit of our achievement, but he believed at the time and still believed that I made a mistake in taking a party to Denmark. I would still argue that if I had conducted myself with more restraint and decorum, our report would have made little impact when it was finally produced.

I must not forget to mention one unlooked-for benefit that followed our inquiry. The best friend that I have made since the war – Major Matthew Oliver, war hero – joined us as an investigator of the criminal aspects of pornography. He uncovered a distressing amount of corruption in the police who were supposed to be prosecuting pornography. Some of them paid a penalty. Matthew and his wife Vivienne have entertained me many times since at St Leonard's. I have described Matt as the most severe critic of my books.

Was it all worthwhile? What harm does pornography, however you define it, actually do? You will never prove coercively that any particular piece of alleged pornography depraves and corrupts. But as I said in that first debate in the Lords, a diet of filth degrades the nation. Again, no one can prove coercively that we had a short or long-term effect. But I am myself certain that we at least stemmed the tide that was flowing strongly in a pornographic direction.

The Bishop of Leicester, one of our eminent members, initiated a debate on our report in the Lords. The majority of the speakers were favourable, as they had been in the earlier debate, but one must not take that at face value. When any topic of general interest is raised – the environment, or dogs for instance – the supporters of the motion tend to outnumber the opponents.

I hope that my deeply admired friend Arnold Goodman will forgive the following reminiscences. With his usual foresight he had arranged to speak *after* me. He was at the time certainly the most amusing and one of the most effective speakers in the House. Without too careful a study of the report he could rely on his debating skill to place it in an unfavourable light. But after the debate started, Eric Fletcher, a member of the committee who was down to speak later, came to me and asked to change places as he had to leave early. So I spoke after Arnold. Arnold was visibly disconcerted, but with his usual generosity of spirit came up to me afterwards and said, 'I have been worked over by a master of the art.'

The whole business certainly brought me to the attention of the tabloid press which, however, was not then such a power in the land as it is today. I am glad to have met Mr Murdoch – a very charming, Oxford-educated Australian whose significance I hardly realised at the time.

They may not like me to say this, but I suppose that I have acquired a kind of special relationship with the *Sun*. They were very contemptuous of me for many years, my friendship with Myra Hindley being one particular object of scorn. In the last year it has been necessary for me to collect the *Sun* daily from the newsagents and point out any passages relating to royalty – most of them far from agreeable – to enable Elizabeth to complete her scholarly work on the monarchy.

No one can deny the paper's readability. I told my friend Jane Reid, a high person in News International, that I thought I was the only member of the Lords that read the *Sun*. She said, 'They all read it, but they cover it up with *The Times.*'

There came a moment when the *Sun* published a statement I felt bound to take up with them. They said there were some crimes that could not be forgiven. I wrote to the editor, Kelvin MacKenzie, whom I had met once before and identified as a humorous character, enclosing a copy of my small book on *Forgiveness*, to help him improve his perspectives. I told him also that I was aware that Mr and Mrs Murdoch were good Christians; how did the *Sun* stand in regard to Christianity?

He accepted an invitation to lunch, while explaining that he disagreed with me totally on forgiveness and, I would think, most things. I was looking forward very much to the lunch. About an hour before it was due to take place I got a message asking if he could bring Mr Davis with him. I was a little bit surprised, because he had insisted earlier that he wanted the lunch to be confined to me and him. Of course I acquiesced. But I waited and waited and there was no sign of Mr MacKenzie or Mr Davis. When I rang up Mr MacKenzie's obviously very efficient secretary she told me that they were coming back to the office because they couldn't find me. In my forty-eight years' experience no one else has ever failed to find me or any other peer in the lobby at the House of Lords.

Today there is plenty of criticism of the tabloids among the so-called educated classes. There is widespread disagreement as to what is their worst feature. For my part, I find most unpleasant of all the comments so widely disseminated about anyone who occupies a high position, whether in politics, royal circles, or elsewhere. This defect, however, is not confined to the tabloids. In 1971 when the press turned its attention on me over pornography, Harold Evans, editor of the *Sunday Times*, warned me, 'Now you're in the news and you must expect more nasty comments than nice.' I realise also that like other frail human beings I am liable to obtain an illicit satisfaction from reading about the weaknesses of my superiors. If I had had the opportunity of putting these points to Mr MacKenzie at luncheon, it may well be that he would have asked me to look in a looking glass.

To turn back for a moment to the problem of pornography, I am not suggesting for a moment that everything unattractive to me or to vast numbers of others should be suppressed, but almost everyone agrees that a line should be drawn *somewhere*. I subscribe to the belief that the situation could be improved by fresh legislation. But in the end public opinion must be brought to bear on those who make such large profits from exploiting our weakness. Suppose that those who have fought the battle against pornography much more strenuously than I have for many years were asked the question: If you could clean up the press or clean up television, which would you clean up first? I am sure that their unhesitating reply would be 'Clean up television'.

For my own part, I must admit that there was a lot of truth in Cecil King's comment that it was 'not my scene'. As I have said, my distaste for pornography is so total that the task of investigating it objectively would always be beyond me. But if not me, who else was likely to have attempted the task? Only Mary Whitehouse is fully committed – and she stands on a pinnacle in this regard. My own remark about myself made in some programme at the time still strikes me as just. 'I am much happier taking up the cudgels on behalf of the stricken. In the end I feel that my vocation lies there rather than in the denunciation of evil. I am not necessarily very good at loving sinners, but I think perhaps I am better at that than at hating the sin.' I would like to leave the last comment on our investigation with the famous Catholic psychiatrist Jack Dominion. He described it as a 'gallant endeavour'.

20
PENAL REFORM

By 1964, as the reader is aware, I was already deeply involved in penal matters. I had begun to visit prisoners in Oxford in the late 1930s. In the mid-fifties I opened the first Lords debate on prisons, initiated with others the New Bridge for ex-prisoners, and published a book on the causes of crime. In 1961 I published a small volume called *The Idea of Punishment*. In 1964 I took the chair of a committee set up by the lawyers' society, Justice, on the victims of crime, and in the same year opened the first Lords' debate on that subject. In that same year, I was chairman of an official Labour Party committee which produced a systematic programme of penal reform. The main items, such as the abolition of capital punishment and the introduction of parole, were carried into law during the Wilson government. Since 1968 I have fully maintained my penal activity. In 1991 I published *Punishment and the Punished*; in 1992, *Prisoner or Patient*, a study of mentally disordered offenders, and in 1993, *Young Offenders*. I have tried to maintain an average of visiting one prison or special hospital a week, sometimes visiting several prisoners at a time, and have maintained a large correspondence with prisoners.

Towards the end of 1968 Myra Hindley, then in her middle twenties, wrote and asked me to call on her. I was astonished to find that the peroxided gorgon of the tabloids was in fact a nice-looking, dark, well-behaved young person. She was desperately anxious to be allowed to meet Ian Brady with whom she was still infatuated or, to use kinder words, deeply in love. In my arguments with the Home Office I seldom believe them to be in the right, but they were absolutely right to refuse to permit a meeting.

People have sometimes asserted that I converted Myra to Roman Catholicism, but that was far from the case. She had been baptised a Catholic. She was not brought up as one, but in her teens she became strongly religious. Then it fell to her lot to work in an office under Ian Brady, who was a few years older than her. Having visited him subsequently over a period of many years, I have no doubt that he was powerfully, almost hypnotically attractive. At any rate, Myra went along with him as an accomplice in the appalling Moors murders; something which would cause her heartbreak for the rest of her life. Myra Hindley has never while in prison shown any signs of violence or cruelty. She has won the respect of many who have visited her, including my wife, David Astor and his wife, and the Reverend Peter Timms, a former governor of Maidstone Prison. A succession of Catholic priests have recognised her deep religious sincerity and have permitted her on occasion to administer the host. She has obtained an honours degree through the Open University.

I hardly expected that Ian Brady would be happy to meet me. It was bound to seem to him that I was an influence on Myra of a religious kind that would militate against their friendship. I doubt if in fact I had much influence of that kind. It is true, however, that gradually, as her religious life developed, a gulf came to yawn between them and they have not been in touch for many years.

Ian Brady is a man of natural intellectuality. It is almost incredible that someone brought up in a very poor area, not knowing who his father was, packed off at one point to Borstal, should, by the time he went to prison, have developed such an impressive knowledge of writers like Dostoevsky, Tolstoy and Blake. When I look back at his earlier letters, I am still astounded at the contrast between this young man of genuine culture and idealism and the author of such dreadful crimes. To give his flavour I will quote one passage:

Incidentally, when I use the word 'redemption', I mean purity of conscience not the, to my mind, narrower theological sense. There are so many paradoxes in the subject of Suffering, and the mind gets caught up in a chicken-and-egg situation. Suffering is, I think, a catalyst of higher Awareness, of self and others and Awareness is Life. But there are so many different combinations of the nature and degree of Awareness, that it is impossible, in my opinion, to decide whether suffering produces more good than evil; but at least we're sure (at least, I am) it certainly produces both good and evil, so is therefore neither completely one nor completely the other.

It was obvious from the beginning that Brady was in some way mentally afflicted. Soon after I got to know him, the Home Secretary, Reginald Maudling, agreed that he should be transferred to hospital. This was blocked by the Minister of Health of the day, apparently on the advice of the Broadmoor authorities. Many years later it was at last conceded that he should be transferred to a special hospital which I had consistently pressed for and which he certainly desired. For some time he has been in Park Lane, now part of Ashworth Hospital, near Liverpool. Sadly, however, he does not wish to see me any more. I shall go on praying for him and Myra, as for so many others in prison and mental hospitals.

I continued to speak regularly on penal matters in the Lords, and to visit prisoners. I became part of a group that worked independently of each other, but at the same time brought concerted pressure to bear on the government in favour of better treatment for prisoners. I have in mind particularly Lord Hunt, of Everest fame, the first chairman of the Parole Board; Lord Donaldson, Secretary of the Pakenham/Thompson Committee, now president of NACRO (National Association for the Care and Resettlement of Offenders) and devoted friend of Grendon Underwood; Lord Hutchinson, the leading criminal barrister of his time; Lord Harris, Minister of State at the Home Office and chairman of the Parole Board; and, above all in the Lords, Baroness Faithfull, former director of Oxford Social Services, already referred to as my 'Conservative mole of compassion'. Lord Windlesham, former Minister of State at the Home Office and chairman of the Parole Board, as well as author of a first-class book on these matters, and Lord Henderson, former Clerk of Parliaments and now President of the New Bridge, have both spoken effectively on penal matters time and again.

Among newcomers to the House, Ann, Baroness Mallalieu, QC, already mentioned, still in her forties – young, by our standards – has given new impulse to penal improvement, and Jane Ewart-Biggs, as I have already explained, brought a graceful distinction to her five years in the chair for the New Bridge.

Much public attention was roused and has never quite died down, by my known friendship with Myra Hindley and Ian Brady. I used to be stopped in the street by unpleasant characters posing the question, 'What about that . . . Myra Hindley?' The most effective reply, I came to find, was to ask, 'Are you a Christian?' The interlocutor would become visibly agitated and stutter out, 'What's that got to do with it?' I would press the issue: 'Do you go to church? Do you say your prayers daily?' With any luck, by that stage, he or she would have made off.

Nevertheless I was conscious of the agony of the relatives of the Moors victims, and indeed many others. I set up a committee of inquiry into the whole issue and brought forward a Bill to improve the treatment of victims. It received a second reading in the Lords. Further progress was not possible at that time. A considerable improvement, though it is still inadequate, has been made since then by government and voluntary bodies in the way victims are treated. I am asked, however, whether I visit victims as often as I visit prisoners. The answer must be no, because neither they, nor their relatives, approach me to anything like the same extent. That may be partly my fault, but I have learnt by now that victims are not usually anxious to parade their sorrows in public.

Over the years I have come to know many prisoners whom I call my friends: Roy Carne, longer than anyone; David Rundall and John Masterson, almost as long. A few days before writing these lines I visited three prisoners in the fairly new Whitemore Prison in Cambridgeshire. They were Dennis

Nilsen, convicted of a dozen murders, Brian Balderstone, convicted of raping his granddaughter, and Frank Beck, serving five life sentences for assaults on young people in the children's homes of which he was in charge.

It is impossible to put a label on Dennis Nilsen. Most people hearing about his crimes, and the way he kept the bodies of his victims in his flat, would say he must be a mental case. However, he has not been sent to hospital and does not wish to be treated as a 'nutter'. He is a tall, well-built man whom one can well believe served for a dozen years in the army.

At the present time he maintains his self-respect in prison in various creative ways. He composes music. I have visited him several times, and described him in my book *Prisoner or Patient*, in which I quote a poem he composed in my honour. On the occasion of my last visit (August 1993) he was understandably annoyed because two video tapes of his musical composition had not been produced for a young man visiting him to take away.

I break off to say that the failure of communications in British prisons is something too familiar to those in welfare and those who visit them. The day after I visited Nilsen at Whitemore I spent an hour waiting to see two prisoners who I had been told would be available at the time I arrived (2PM). The excuses were unrefutably feeble, but as always I found it difficult to blame any individual. One day someone will look into the whole question of these internal communications in prison. I shall be surprised if they do not reach the conclusion that the governors ought to be much more present, in the manner of the efficient business managers today.

Dennis Nilsen has an excellent sense of humour. I told him that I admired the way he had developed his talents, writing music, painting and, as I learned from an education officer, writing excellent essays. 'I am completely self taught,' he replied. 'I left school at fifteen.' I could not help remarking that John Major left school without O levels when he was not much older. I looked round the room at Whitemore Prison and commented, 'He seems to have got further than you or me.' Nilsen thoroughly enjoyed the joke.

If I am asked if he feels remorse, I mention this: Ruth

Rendell, the famous crime writer, is publishing an anthology of murder and is very pleased with a contribution by Nilsen which I obtained for her. When offered a fee he declined because it 'would have been blood money'. Dennis Nilsen does not show remorse. But having visited him half a dozen times I know that he will always feel it. I mentioned forgiveness to him. He told me, 'No one can forgive except my victims, and they are dead.' I said, 'If you are going to believe in God you will realise that He will and can forgive you.' Des, as we call him, is not as yet religious. But 'perhaps before the end some light will shine', to quote from the autobiography of Lady Diana Cooper.

As far as Brian Balderstone is concerned, I wish he were out of prison by the time these words are published. He has difficulties with remorse. At the time of his offences he was a Mormon priest; now he receives much consolation from the pentecostals. He and his wife used to have one of his granddaughters in bed with them, and he was convicted of serious offences against his granddaughter. He does not admit to rape, but recognises he behaved improperly. When he is released he hopes to live in a Christian hostel. I promised to write to his former employer about his future.

The third prisoner I visited on that occasion was Frank Beck, who was convicted of a whole series of offences in the children's homes he was in charge of under Leicestershire County Council for thirteen years. On the face of it his is a dreadful story. He is, however, appealing against the convictions, although I gather the appeal will not be heard possibly until later in 1994. I am now, after several visits, personally convinced of his total innocence. He made an excellent first impression on me, and again impressed me the second time I visited, when he had two solicitors present so that we had a very detailed discussion. On this second occasion he reminded me that I had told the press he had honest eyes; certainly I would confirm that assessment.

By the time this book is published his case may well have come to appeal, but I must write as I see his situation and personality today, 17 September 1993.

I have never come across a case like his; the facts seem to be in total contradiction to each other. I extract the following statements from the report of an inquiry into the management of children's homes in Leicestershire during 1973 by Andrew Kirkwood QC.

In 1973 Mr Frank Beck, a former Royal Marines sergeant and a single man, fresh from Stevenage College of Further Education where he had obtained the qualification CQSW, was appointed Officer in Charge of a Children's Home in Market Harborough in Leicestershire. He remained in the employment of Leicestershire County Council as Officer in Charge of Children's Homes until his resignation in March 1986 . . .

In 1982, after nine years' employment by Leicestershire County Council, Frank Beck applied for approval as a foster parent. He was approved to foster a teenager in 1983 and given general approval as a foster parent in 1984. It must be assumed that by this time the authority and its various officials had a close knowledge of Mr Beck's methods and conduct. On 12th August 1982, Dr Carter, the consultant psychiatrist who provided staff consultation at the Beeches where Mr Beck was employed, backed his application for fostering as follows: 'I have known Frank for the last three-and-a-half years through my regular weekly consultation at the Beeches Children and Family Centre.' He went on to say that he was aware of suggestions among 'fieldworkers that Frank was homosexual' but concluded, 'I have a uniformly high opinion of Frank. I believe he would manage a fostering situation with this sixteen-year-old boy in an appropriate and useful fashion.' It was concluded when he applied for a general fostering permission that 'as far as PQ, the boy in question, is concerned, the fostering placement has been a success'. The supervising officer has been impressed by Mr Beck's awareness of the many issues involved and his adjustment in accepting a parental role, set against his role at the Beeches.

Any fair-minded juryman ought surely to have been impressed that Frank Beck's two foster children spoke up strongly for him at his trial.

Frank Beck resigned from service with Leicestershire County Council in 1986 under somewhat controversial circumstances. The fact is that those who had every opportunity of examining his work from 1973 to 1984 formed a very high opinion of him.

In 1989 a Mrs Outhwait, who had been in residential care at one of his homes as a teenager, began to tell her family social worker of her alleged experiences while in Mr Beck's charge. In May 1990 Frank Beck and three other men were arrested. Frank Beck was found guilty on seventeen counts involving sexual and physical assault. These convictions included four offences of buggery and one of rape. Beck was sentenced to life imprisonment for each offence of buggery and rape. He was further sentenced to an aggregate of twenty-four years' imprisonment in respect of other offences. He maintains that he is totally innocent of all these charges and is appealing not only against sentence but conviction.

On the face of it, it is almost unbelievable that if he was breaking the law in this horrendous way for all those years he could be approved by the local authority with their various opportunities of inspection. Can one begin to understand how such a tragic situation could arise? I have not yet mentioned that he was from the beginning, with the approval of the authority, engaged in so-called regressive therapy, which involved taking young adolescents back to early childhood and, it may be, feeding them from a bottle. On my third visit, Frank Beck explained to me that regressive therapy was not applied unless children were ready to accept it. At the Beeches it was little used. His whole approach, however, based on what seemed accepted at the time as the best modern thinking, depended on the use of physical contact as a means of transmitting love. When I told Frank that I would not wish any of my children to be submitted to that experience, he pointed out that the children or young persons he was dealing with had been deprived of love up until then, and in that sense they were not typical. However, he and others, I believe, will justify this method of physical contact in the transmission of love.

One day when I was lunching in the Lords there were six

people at a neighbouring table. A middle-aged lady got up to leave and went round solemnly hugging the other guests and the peer who was her host. At the end of lunch, the peer came over to me and said, 'I noticed that you were rather surprised by what you saw. You don't seem to be up-to-date with hug therapy.' I certainly would not wish to pronounce on all such therapeutic methods.

The dangers of such therapy, however, especially to those who have little means of objection, are obvious; it would surely be very difficult to avoid a strong emotional relationship. There is no doubt whatever that Frank Beck was remarkably successful with disturbed children. But much of this success depended on persuading these unloved children that they were loved. Is there no danger that the therapists would go beyond the bounds of propriety and indulge in some sexual relationship? No doubt such matters will be much discussed before the Court of Appeal. Personally I am convinced that not only did Frank Beck act throughout as an idealist but that he did not exceed the bounds of propriety and certainly did not commit any criminal act.

One is bound to face the fact that a number of these children gave evidence against him, though others spoke up in his favour and some have continued to visit him in prison. Those who spoke against him were usually, it would seem, likely to gain financially if he were convicted. A girl whom he was convicted of raping has since been offered large compensation, but at first considered it inadequate. Many young people are said to be putting in claims of money. One of the solicitors handling the appeal told me that where they had been able to obtain the police records of Frank Beck's accusers, these were enough to discredit them. They had not been able to obtain the records at the time of the trial of those whose evidence was accepted by the jury. Since then, however, this information has been extracted from the police. At the time of writing, the former chairman of the Bar Council, Mr Scrimgeour, is leading the appeal, which suggests that the case of Frank Beck possesses no little strength.

Looking at it in the broadest way it would seem to me outrageous if Frank Beck was forced to serve five life sentences for a form of conduct which was approved by his superiors for so many years.

The day after that visit to Nilsen, Balderstone and Beck, I paid another visit to see Eddie Richardson, now in Parkhurst. I had visited Eddie before, at an earlier stage in his life, in more than one prison. He made very good use of his time outside prison; I certainly think that he built up an excellent business. One of his daughters obtained her degree at London University, the other danced in the Royal Ballet. They and his charming wife have been welcomed by me more than once in the House of Lords. Suddenly this blow fell, and he was charged with the importation of drugs (cannabis and cocaine). I gave evidence for him, and asked Counsel how many years he would get. I was told ten or fifteen. I gave evidence to his character and I said, 'I have a great liking for Eddie. I know well that he has a good side.'

The judge was more than deaf to my appeal. He said, 'Your friend says that you have a good side. I am glad to say that you will be able to develop it in the next twenty-five years in prison. You may not realise that by importing illegal drugs you were doing the equivalent of firing a machine-gun into a crowd.' At the moment of writing I regret to say that Eddie has lost his appeal, though ably assisted by Edward Fitzgerald, the brilliant barrister husband of Antonia's eldest child Rebecca, who has, incidentally, already made a name as a biographer.

What is extraordinary about Eddie is that he has become a talented painter in prison, though he had never done any painting before. He did a portrait of me without any sittings which has since been sold for charity. He has had other pictures exhibited, and when I visited the 1993 Koestler exhibition of prisoners' art, one of his pictures had won a major award.

On my way down to Parkhurst Prison, Isle of Wight, I was addressed by a youngish man accompanied by his small son. I could hardly believe it, but he was then serving ten years for armed robbery. While in prison, he has achieved a remarkable reputation as an architectural historian, as this advertisement shows:

THOMAS ARCHER AT HALE

A Baroque Entertainment by Peter Wayne
Saturday 11th September 1993
6.30PM for 7PM

At St Mary's, Hale Park, Hampshire

By kind permission of
Mr and Mrs Patrick Hickman & the Hale PCC

Since then I am glad to see he has been granted parole and is beginning work at the Courtauld Institute. Who can say, therefore, with the stories of Edward Richardson and Peter Wayne in front of them, that prison never affords creative opportunities. But one can never forget that for most prisoners it is a painful, deadening experience.

The problem of mentally disordered offenders has long haunted me. In 1959, a gifted young public relations officer, Peter Thompson, recruited me for a strong representative committee later called the Pakenham Thompson Committee (it would have been better called the Thompson Pakenham Committee) to investigate the question of prison aftercare. Our report, I still think, had an important effect on the development of national policy, though there is still a yawning gap in this area.

Peter later had a total breakdown and spent four years in Broadmoor. When he emerged, I wrote introductions to two of his books. Much more significantly, he has founded and inspired the Matthew Trust for ex-mental patients and victims of crime. I have several times described him in the Lords as doing more for ex-mental patients than any other individual. For the purposes of my book, *Prisoner or Patient*, I visited a large number of mentally disturbed prisoners. I have already referred to Ian Brady; I already knew Ronnie and Reggie Kray, those disparate but equally striking twins, Reggie still in prison, Ronnie in Broadmoor. I had also met Peter Sutcliffe, the so-called 'Ripper', who seemed, I must say, extraordinarily normal. He told me that he still heard the voices which led to

169

his terrible crimes; now with the help of Jehovah's Witnesses he identifies them as coming from the Devil and can disregard them. On the other hand, Dennis Nilsen, whom many would regard as a psychiatric case, wishes, as I have already mentioned, to remain in prison, rather than go to hospital.

In the end we are relying on the advice of psychiatrists. They are not infallible, but we must do the best we can. The decision whether to transfer a prisoner to a mental hospital or to release him from that hospital must always involve an element of risk. The decision is made much more difficult by our failure to provide community care on anything like the scale required.

Young offenders – those under twenty-one – are a different problem again. For a long time in Britain there has been general agreement that they should be treated differently; in other words, in a more constructive fashion than adults. It would be impossible to say that this rule is at present applied in young offenders' institutions, in spite of the heroic exertions, for example, of Jo Whitty, till recently Governor of Feltham. One large development must be placed on the credit side. The number of those over twenty-one in custody has increased along with the increase in crime, if not so rapidly. The number of those under twenty-one has been much diminished. There is no sign that lighter sentences have led to a relative increase in offending by young people. Penal reformers like myself are entitled to argue that there is an obvious moral here in regard to the treatment of adults. One has to admit, however, that the statistics involved are so unsatisfactory that such pronouncements can only be made with caution.

In March 1993, Kenneth Clarke, then Home Secretary, announced an important new initiative in regard to young offenders. The main feature was the proposed establishment of a small number (possibly five) of secure units for young offenders of twelve, thirteen, fourteen and fifteen (possibly forty in each unit). This proposal was part of a wider scheme to increase discipline in schools and children's homes through the agency of the Department of Education and the Department of Health.

The proposals were immediately denounced by leading

penal reform and children's organisations. There was, indeed, widespread criticism in serious quarters. A heading in a *Times* leading article was typical of many: 'Panic over Crime'. The government's new policy has been hastily conceived.

The Times recognised the public alarm as being a result of the horrific murder of a two-year-old boy by two boys of ten and eleven. Since then a judge has decided (his decision was later overruled) not to send a fifteen-year-old rapist into protective custody. Soon after Mr Clarke's statement a schoolteacher was raped by a boy of thirteen with the assistance of a boy of fourteen. *The Times* responded as follows: 'One horrific child murder does not make a crime wave . . .Yesterday's statement of juvenile crime . . . had all the hallmarks of a policy both conceived and announced in panic.'

More recently, Virginia Bottomley, Minister of Health, has announced that she is setting up institutions which sound remarkably similar to Mr Clarke's.

I must make it plain that I am not as opposed as some of my penal reform colleagues to removing some persistent offenders, or some who have committed very grave crimes, from home. But the places of custody should be educational and therapeutic. They should in no case come under the Home Office and least of all be privatised.

And never let us forget, if we are really concerned with the reform or education or therapy of prisoners or young offenders, what we do when they emerge from custody is at least as important as what we do for them while they are in custody.

More recently still, Kenneth Clarke's successor as Home Secretary, Michael Howard, has sought to inaugurate a new era in penal history, assuming, in his own eyes, a new initiative in the war against crime. His speech to the Conservative conference in October 1993 was greeted with heartfelt applause by the delegates, but denounced by representatives of all those concerned directly with the treatment of prisoners from the judiciary to prison officers, not to mention penal reformers.

The views of the prisoners were, it would seem, unprintable.

With his Criminal Justice Bill and his Police Bill, Mr Howard has also managed to antagonise such bodies as the Bar Council and the Law Society, never mind the police; this will hardly be helpful to him in his pursuit of law and order.

Much attention has centred on his proposal to set up five new secure units for persistent, or very serious young offenders. This is in essence Mr Clarke's proposal. Mr Howard has dropped the age to ten but reduced the period of maximum detention from two years to one. I am just as strongly opposed to his approach as to his predecessor's.

As I write, the struggle continues in the Lords.

After more than fifty years of involvement with prisons and prisoners many reflections are inevitable. I will offer only a few. When I became a prison visitor in the late thirties, there were 10,000 people in prison. Now there are about to be 50,000 with a further increase expected. The remorseless increase in crime is by and large responsible. In the view, however, of all penal reformers, we send far too many people to prison in this country. We continue to send more per head of the population than any other European country. As I have said as strongly as I have been able to in the House of Lords, we shall never correct that tendency until we have a sentencing council which can exercise a moderating influence on the judiciary.

It is difficult to distinguish the treatment of prisoners from the sentencing of prisoners, because treatment depends so much on the numbers in prison in relation to staff and buildings. It is impossible to exaggerate the dedication of countless members of the prison service and others working beside them. There will always be a tension between the conception of prison as a form of punishment aimed at deterrence and prison as a means of reforming wrongdoers. Penal reformers like myself find it easy to state the elements of a just sentence; deterrence, reform, retribution (or fairness) and prevention – that is to say, keeping wrongdoers where they can do little harm. In practice, the tide of penal reform ebbs and flows. Logical reasons do not always influence policy.

Following the Strangeways riots, an historic report was published over the names of Lord Justice Woolf and Judge Stephen Tumim. To a considerable extent it inspired the

Criminal Justice Act of 1991 although, like many other penal reformers, I do not believe that we shall ever reduce our prison population as we should without a sentencing council. But Lord Windlesham, now Principal of Brasenose College, Oxford, published in 1993 a notable book in which he laments the retrograde changes already beginning to be made in the Act of 1991.

At the present moment the prospect looks still worse with the new Home Secretary favouring widespread privatisation. Privatisation I have denounced in the Lords and will denounce again. Privatisation is a real obscenity. The idea of handing over helpless prisoners or young offenders to commercial bodies whose driving force is a search for profit must surely be anathema to all who think it over carefully.

To sum up my attitude: if anyone asks me, 'Have you anything in common with someone who has been convicted of a series of terrible crimes?' I reply, 'I have everything in common with him or her. He or she is a member of the human race as much as I am.'

I would like to draw attention to a speech made by Lord Elton on 8 December 1993 in the House of Lords, where he rose to call attention to the conditions necessary for the maintenance in the citizens of this country of a proper respect for each other and for the law. In essence, he was trying to distinguish a fundamental approach to crime and criminals which would be acceptable to men and women of all parties or none. At the deepest level he found the answer in the age-long Christian injunction to love our neighbours.

Lord Elton is well equipped to propound such a thesis. He was a Conservative Minister of State at the Home Office (as was another devout Christian, Lord Windlesham). Since leaving office he has played a prominent part in the field of alternative remedies to prison, and in Christian initiatives.

For many years across the floor of the House, and indeed as recently as 1 December 1993, I have differed from Rodney Elton quite sharply in regard to particular policies. But there are things deeper than politics. I wholeheartedly agree with him in this instance, as would Christians and many non-

Christians from all quarters of the House, and countless men and women in humbler circumstances. We know well that if we could somehow manage to love our neighbour more adequately, there would be little talk of crime. We citizens are entitled to call on our political leaders to prove worthy of their position and give a moral lead. But we cannot escape our own duty, which is to set an example in our own lives.

Addendum:
While this book was going to press ,the Criminal Justice Bill of 1993 was going through the House of Lords. I have made my contribution, not a major one, to the prolonged debates. I cannot pretend that it will add to human welfare, but as always in penal affairs I cling to the motto, 'Tomorrow is also a day'.

21
BOOKS

It seems extraordinary to me now that I should have written twenty-six books on my own, and two for which more than half the work was done by a partner. Nine were on religion, five on penal affairs, four were of an autobiographical nature and three on Ireland (it was on two of these that the main work was done by my colleagues). On all these matters my views will have emerged by the end of the present volume. I have also written a history of the House of Lords. That leaves a book called *Peacemakers*, three which were lives of American presidents, and *Eleven at Number Ten*, an account of the eleven prime ministers preceding John Major. *Peacemakers* must be seen today as a product of the Cold War period, now finished; but I drew considerably on my experience as a lecturer on international history and international relations before the war. Looking back I am glad that I tried to do justice to the Greenham Common women, whom I visited during their freezing vigil, and Bruce Kent, then chairman of CND.

When I interviewed him for the book, Bruce Kent was still a priest, whom I addressed as Father. Perhaps it should have been Monseigneur. He commented, 'When we all lived in Golders Green your wife asked me to go to a Catholic ball with my contemporary Antonia, then about to "come out". Unfortunately I had to decline, otherwise it might have been me calling you father.'

175

I wrote books about Abraham Lincoln, John Kennedy and Richard Nixon. Of these the Lincoln biography was the most substantial. None of them was lengthy by the standards of my family's books. In August 1993 I was flattered to be invited by a distinguished American society to rededicate the statue to Abraham Lincoln put up in Edinburgh a hundred years before. It was raised in memory of the Scotsmen who laid down their lives in Lincoln's army. I had to confess to feeling something of an impostor in front of a distinguished gathering of American visitors and Edinburgh notables presided over by the Lord Provost. I admitted that my six Scottish grandchildren (Frasers) were hardly a full justification. I plucked up courage, however, and consoled myself with the thought that my book on Lincoln must have found a measure of approval in expert American eyes.

Its introduction was written by Elizabeth, who began by saying, 'Taken together, Abraham Lincoln's life and death formed the perfect pattern for a national hero. From the valleys to the peaks and back to the valley – of sudden death.' My own opening words were:

> As the nineteenth century recedes from us, Abraham Lincoln stands out ever more incontestably above all other American statesmen. In the whole of modern political history one cannot readily point to his superior; it is difficult even to suggest his equal. We pay tribute to his moral grandeur, his triumphant prosecution of noble causes and his extraordinary gift of words, eloquent, humorous and tender.

Let me try to be a little more analytical in distinguishing the elements of Lincoln's greatness, even if those elements are somewhat overlapping.

Lincoln himself said, in August 1862, at the height of the Civil War, 'My paramount object in this struggle is to save the Union. I shall do less whenever I believe what I am doing hurts the cause and I shall do more whenever I shall believe doing more will help the cause.' For such a cause, one could imagine vast numbers of Americans laying down their lives, but Lincoln surely stands for something more universal.

I was once told that Lincoln appeals particularly to Scotsmen as a self-made man. There have been six Scottish prime ministers this century – H.A. Balfour, Campbell Bannerman, Bonar Law, Ramsay MacDonald, Harold Macmillan and Alec Home. Of those, Bonar Law might be said to be relatively self-made compared to the others, but only Ramsay MacDonald began life at the very bottom like Abraham Lincoln. Lincoln's father, as I say in my book, was 'a failure in life by any ordinary standard'. There was a steady retrogression in his later years. Eventually he seems to have forgotten how to write his name. Does one admire Abraham Lincoln all the more? Do we admire, for example, John Major more than Alec Home because one came from nowhere and the other was born with a golden spoon in his mouth? I leave it to you to judge, but it is not my own main reason for admiring Lincoln. Others will say, and rightly, that he was the greatest exponent of the democratic ideal that ever lived. I must be forgiven for repeating yet again the immortal words, 'We here highly resolve that these men shall not have died in vain.'

I shall not become embroiled in the question of whether it is right to see Lincoln as the supreme emancipator of the slaves. For my part, I shall always see him in that light, even if he came out for full emancipation a good deal later than some. After his Second Inaugural, in January 1865, Douglas, the Negro leader, came up to him and said, 'Mr Lincoln, that was a sacred thing.' Lincoln had the perfect answer: 'I am glad you like it,' he told Douglas.

But what a speech that was; arguably the greatest political speech ever delivered, bearing in mind the situation. Lincoln was on the point of total victory, a situation in which conquerors have seldom if ever shown magnanimity. Of the two sides in the Civil War, then drawing to a close, he had this to say: 'Both read the same Bible and pray to the same God. And each invokes His aid against the other. The prayers of both could not be answered. That of neither has been answered fully. With firmness in the right, as God gives us to see the right, let us strive on to finish the work we're in.'

Did anyone ever show so much understanding to those

facing total defeat, and so much personal humility? Was Lincoln by the end of his life a Christian? We need have no doubts on that score. To quote his own words: 'When I left Springfield, I asked the people to pray for me. I was not a Christian. When I buried my son, the severest trial of my life, in 1862, I was not a Christian. But when I went to Gettysburg and saw the graves of thousands of our soldiers, I then and there consecrated myself to Christ.'

For me, the most moving expression of Lincoln's fundamental personality is to be found in a letter he wrote to the daughter of one of his colonels. The officer had been killed, and his daughter was inconsolable. I can only quote a small part of it now; we must remember that it was written at Christmas, 1862, when he was, one might have thought, totally absorbed in grave anxieties.

'It is with deep grief', he wrote, 'that I learn of the death of your kind and brave father; and especially that it is affecting your young heart beyond what is common in such cases . . . You cannot now realise that you will ever feel better. Is not this so? And yet it is a mistake. You are sure to be happy again . . . The memory of your dear father, instead of an agony, will yet be a sad sweet feeling in your heart of a purer and holier sort than you have ever known before.'

Nothing said about Lincoln can ever improve on what he said and did himself.

I take no particular pride in my life of Jack Kennedy, although I am glad to have spent, so to speak, a little time in his company. I met him once when he was the guest of President de Valera in Phoenix Park, Dublin. I knew that he had long been a close friend of my son-in-law Hugh Fraser, from the time when his father was American ambassador in London, and I was gratified at his evident pleasure at the mention of the name of my daughter Antonia. 'Antonia,' he repeated excitedly, 'Antonia Fraser.' Not perhaps a very memorable conversation with the President, but very pleasant all the same. At a discreet distance I followed him around the President's lawn all the afternoon and observed his magic at work in contact after contact. It did indeed seem that the native Irishman had returned.

When I wrote my book about Kennedy I was still enthusiastically reacting to the election of a Catholic as President of the United States. I am still happy to think that this occurred, although I could wish that his private life had not been so irregular by Catholic standards.

When I was writing about him I interviewed Harold Macmillan at Birch Grove, and I asked whether it was true as reported that President Kennedy had asked to be supplied with a woman a day during his visit to the British Prime Minister. It was said that he would otherwise suffer from acute headaches. Harold Macmillan dealt with the suggestion superbly. 'Oh no,' he said, 'Jack would never have done that. Jack had such beautiful manners. He would have thought talking about sex to me was like talking about sex to one's father.' Bearing in mind the reputation in that area of Joe Kennedy, the comment was perhaps more ambiguous than I realised.

Since then I have always reminded myself, when tending to be over-critical about Jack Kennedy's private life, that he was suffering constant pain from his war injuries. At the end of my book I used a quotation from John Buchan's *The Halfhearted*: 'This man was of the race of kings.' Jack Kennedy was by my standards still a young man. I do not put aside the inspiration that he provided to the free world during his presidency. I cherish the supposition that he might have, in spite of certain personal weaknesses, achieved greatness.

I am much happier to think of what I wrote about Richard Nixon. I saw quite a lot of him on two of his visits to London. Sidgwick & Jackson published two of his books and I took the chair for him twice in front of expert and indeed critical audiences. On each occasion he showed a prodigious grasp of world affairs. I am interested to read, in the fine biography of him by Jonathan Aitken, that he was also deeply impressed in the same way. I admire Nixon most, however, for his recovery from the depths of discredit.

At the moment of his resignation, disgraced as no other president this century, he announced his determination on no account to be bitter. His rehabilitation is a source of tremendous pleasure to me, and to so many who were close to him. He was kind enough to send me his last book of memoirs.

Near the end he records, in the old Quaker phrase of his childhood, 'I have found peace at the centre.' Who will deny that by the end of his life he deserved it.

Eleven at Number Ten consists of essays on the eleven prime ministers before John Major. I have known them all – some only slightly, others quite well. Baldwin, Chamberlain, Churchill, Attlee and Wilson have already figured in this book. I provide below a few personal comments on the others.

Anthony Eden has been delineated by Nico Henderson as an aesthete, soldier, statesman. I was once speaking with Eden at a United Nations rally at Warwick Castle. 'I never can forget', he began and then collapsed. He pluckily resumed. 'I never can forget', he began again and then collapsed again on the grass beside me. Once again he rose and resumed his speech. For the third time he collapsed. I caught him as he fell, noting how light he was for such a tall, well-built man. Again he rose but this time our host, the Earl of Warwick, intervened and Eden was persuaded to leave the rostrum. After tea he set off to make a speech elsewhere. On the following morning he carried out a whole programme of public engagements. From then on I never doubted two things: the precariousness of his health and the unlimited gallantry with which he would face disaster. His Suez initiative admittedly surprised me, but not his infinitely brave response to the tragedy.

He was succeeded by Harold Macmillan; 'first in and first out', as he used to say of his role in regard to Suez. When I first met him shortly before the war, we were both staying with his brother-in-law, the Duke of Devonshire, at Compton Place near Eastbourne. At that time Macmillan was regarded as a high-class maverick: Balliol, gallant war service in the Guards, married to a duke's daughter, a very rich publisher but, in his middle forties, 'on the beach' politically. Indeed, during the house party in question, he discussed with me the possibility of joining the Labour Party. He had already written a book called *The Middle Way*. He came down definitely against such a move. 'After all,' he reflected, 'I am a very rich man.' I am not implying that he thought that he would suffer under a Labour government, but that with his ever-present sense of history, he felt the absurdity of such a role.

No one in those days questioned his integrity or mental powers. He had obtained a first-class honours Moderations at Oxford, and if it had not been for the war I feel sure that he would have obtained a first in Greats. But in middle life Harold Macmillan, so I am told, was regarded as rather a bore in sophisticated circles. By his nineties he had developed histrionic genius. The Lords were spellbound by his speech deriding Mrs Thatcher's government for selling the family silver. I remember still more vividly a speech he delivered to not more than a dozen guests, as Chancellor of Oxford, at St Benet's House.

'I remember so well', he told us, 'my first night away from home at the school up the road there' (he pretended to have forgotten the name but everyone knew it was coming) 'Summerfields. I was crying myself to sleep, when a boy in the next bed (here he took us into his confidence), Evelyn Baring, said to me, "Don't cry, little boy, your position is bad but not hopeless."' Then the orator really took off. 'And so it is with our beloved country.'

Alec Home is recognised as a great gentleman of politics. At Eton he was the outstanding cricketer of his year, a fine all-round athlete and President of Pop; a glamour figure, if ever there was one at the school. Two-and-a-half years younger, and in a different House, I would never have dared to speak to him. It was not till he married a very clever daughter of the headmaster, Dr Alington, that I began to recognise his intellectual qualities. No husband and wife were ever more wrapped up in each other.

Prime ministers are, to say the least, chary of serving under their successors. Asquith considered it unthinkable that he should serve under Lloyd George; one cannot imagine Ted Heath serving under Margaret Thatcher, and having recently heard Margaret Thatcher lead her revolt in the House of Lords against Maastricht, I cannot visualise her in John Major's cabinet. Alec Home served loyally and effectively under Ted Heath as Foreign Secretary. I understand from a close friend that he was genuinely reluctant to accept the position, but did

181

so out of a sheer sense of duty. The death of his wife, Elizabeth, was a tremendous blow. He is not now well enough to attend the Lords, but his name is still mentioned there with a kind of reverence given to few politicians.

Ted Heath I have described as a big man with a little side; an impressive unauthorised biography has described him as a Shakespearean tragic hero. The biographer expresses the opinion that Heath's reputation, damaged, one must admit, by his attitude to his successor, is beginning to be restored.

As I explained, Sidgwick published successful books by Ted Heath on sailing, music and travel. For myself, I think of him most of all as a man of music. When I saw him at close quarters conducting the London Symphony Orchestra, he was transformed. I can't resist, however, supplying an illustration of his sharp tongue. One day it was announced in the newspapers that he had lost a stone in weight by careful dieting. I found myself standing next to him at a function at the Savoy. 'Hello, Ted,' I said, 'how's the weight?' 'All right,' he said coldly, 'how's yours?'

In my dealings with him, as chairman of his publishers, I found him invariably considerate and courteous and a superlative speaker at launching functions.

Margaret Thatcher, the next incumbent, has provided in Thatcherism the only social philosophy associated with a prime minister. I would not put Gladstonian Liberalism on the same footing.

Many of my left-wing colleagues are severe critics of Baroness Thatcher. I am not among her extreme opponents. In June 1970, after it was known that the Conservatives had won the election, I ran into her at our local newsagent. Bearing in mind my own experience, I said, 'I suppose that you'll be sitting by the telephone waiting for the summons from No. 10?' She tossed her head. 'I'm not the sort who hangs around by the telephone on such an occasion.' I said, 'But if they want you to become a minister, they'll have to make contact with you.' 'Oh, I've got someone else to look after that side of it.' I assumed she meant Denis.

While she was still Minister of Education she came over to dinner with us at Hurst Green, Sussex. She was then living at

Lamberhurst, a few miles away. Ever since then, should my guests, as I'm afraid they do sometimes, begin criticising her, I point out to the lady on my right that that chair was once occupied by Mrs T. and that next time there will be a tablet erected in her memory.

Denis and I talked about rugger. He was a professional referee. His finest memory was when one of the players committed an offence. Denis said, 'Next time you do that, you'll go off.' The captain came up and remonstrated. Denis said, 'Next time either of you do anything like this, you'll both go off.' This recollection gave him enormous satisfaction. I found him a very sympathetic man.

Margaret Thatcher was very easy to talk to and not unduly dogmatic in those days. I clearly remember one thing she said to me. Another woman, not of her party, was going strong at the time. Margaret said of her, 'She has no power of decision.' I have always realised that this is a quality on which she prided herself before all else, and not without reason.

Many times since then I have denounced Thatcherism in the House of Lords and elsewhere. But I have never doubted that she is a moral woman, who went to chapel several times on Sundays as a girl and, to the best of my belief, is a religious Anglican today. What does Thatcherism, in the last resort, stand for? Self-esteem? Self-respect? Surely these are noble aspirations. But self-interest is more ambiguous, and we on the Left in politics consider that selfishness has been promoted all too effectively in recent years. If, however, we are Christians, we realise it is perfectly possible for Christians to differ on such matters.

I would mention two other qualities Lady Thatcher possesses: self-control and beautiful manners towards strangers. When the interminable debate on Maastricht was getting under way I asked her whether she was going to speak at the Committee stage. She said she was reserving herself for the debate on the referendum, which would not come until near the end. Hour after hour, day after day, she sat there poker-faced. No one could guess what she was thinking. When the day for the referendum arrived, she deliberately waited till nearly seven o'clock, that is to say for four hours, in her place, so that she would be able to follow rather than be followed by her main critics. When she sat down, she had probably not turned over many, or perhaps any, votes in the House, but she had inspired her followers in the Commons, who crowded round the Bar, to keep the fight going.

Shortly before writing this, we entertained to lunch in the Lords an American cousin of my American daughter-in-law, Mimi. Elizabeth spotted Margaret Thatcher two tables away. Edith, the mayor of her home town, said she had met her some years before in St Louis. She did not expect to be remembered. I led her over and introduced her to Margaret Thatcher, who welcomed her as though she were a long-lost sister. At the same time, she gracefully congratulated Elizabeth on her book on the monarchy. Elizabeth was undeniably gratified.

When Margaret Thatcher was disposed of, her place was taken by someone who was extremely well-liked, but whose views were unknown, as indeed they remain. I understand that when a vacancy occurred in the constituency of Huntingdon in 1979, there were 200 applicants to be candidate. John Major had no track record, but he was chosen because of his personal charm.

Recently, I told the story in the Lords of an elderly lady friend of mine who said, 'I like this Mr Major. He hasn't the faintest idea what to do, but he keeps smiling.' More recently still, I had the honour of being received by him at a reception for overseas delegates at 10 Downing Street. His first words surprised me: 'Good to see you, Frank' – though we had never met. I told this with some pride to the next man in the queue, a middle-grade Foreign Office official who also had not met him before. He said, 'He called me Jim.' So it's part of a policy, and although it is easy to mock it, it seems to me to be much more to be admired than otherwise.

After that single encounter, I see him as a man who sets out to be the friend of all the world, and not only when it would be to his obvious advantage. He had nothing to gain from me, or the official. It is said he likes to be liked by everyone. Well, there is no harm in that, though it is not a complete recipe for governing the country.

I began the final chapter of *Eleven at Number Ten* with a quotation from a book called *The Lost Dominion,* an account of the men responsible for the so-called loss of India: 'The question is, *qua mente?* (with what intention) . . . and all these men had noble ideals.' I will say the same of our eleven prime ministers. Without the implication that on balance their performance was a failure. I was derided for saying something so naïve by a well-known journalist in the *Sunday Telegraph.* But I would say the same today, and add the name of John Major. I end with a quotation from the German Chancellor von Bülow: 'Real politicians are animated by two motives only, love of country and love of power.'

I submitted that none of the prime ministers considered was devoid of a substantial personal ambition, though Attlee and Home, and it might be said, Stanley Baldwin, could not be called ambitious men. Today I would rather say of the twelve that they struck a balance – a good balance by human standards – between conscience and ambition.

Later in my concluding chapter I wrote, 'The prime ministers were chosen because the selectors considered that these individuals had the all-round capacity to do the job better than anyone else.' That is almost a platitude. Can I be a little more specific now? I would suggest that to each of them was given some special quality which greatly assisted their achievements. To Baldwin, a profound sense of Britain, or as he usually called it, England. To Chamberlain, a rectitude that carried him to the breaking point and beyond. To Churchill, the one man of genius among them, an incomparable fighting spirit and the capacity to express it in incomparable words. To Attlee, humility and self-esteem, uniquely combined. To Eden, a sensitive chivalry carried to the point of collapse. To Macmillan, an unwearying shrewdness embellished in his last years by superb histrionics. To Home, the virtues associated with a Christian aristocrat. To Wilson, those of a boy scout equipped with an alpha plus intelligence. To Heath, a love of music which gave him a strength beyond that of most politicians. To Callaghan, the best natural eloquence of them all. To Margaret Thatcher, a sense of moral purpose which inspired very many and antagonised not a few. To John Major, a positive friendliness.

185

Each of my books has been completed within a year. I have already written of Gwen Keeble, who helped me so much, Barbara Winch joined me even earlier. She has the exceptional gift of typing very fast and at the same time commenting astutely on the typescript. She and her husband Peter have looked after our little estate for many years, as did Peter's late father. We are deeply indebted to their family.

None of my literary efforts, however, can compare with the noble volumes produced by members of my family. Many years ago I described Elizabeth as having a truer talent than myself and she is not the only member of my family of whom I make that concession. In addition, the time that they spend on most of their books makes me feel ashamed. Elizabeth took four years on her *Queen Victoria* and eight on *Wellington*. Her latest triumph, *Royal Throne,* is admittedly quite short, but it is the fruit of thirty years' study and experience.

Antonia has taken several years over her splendid biographies of Mary Queen of Scots, Oliver Cromwell, Charles II, and her other historical works. She has been awarded three honorary degrees at universities, a feat, I should imagine, unrivalled by any female television star. Her recent *Six Wives of Henry the Eighth* has for month after month been high on the British bestseller list and has also featured on the bestseller list in New York.

Thomas's *History of the Boer War,* ten years in the making, is now a classic, equally admired, I understand, by Presidents de Klerk and Mandela. His *Scramble for Africa,* as I have said, won the W.H. Smith prize. Judith has published five volumes of poetry, well-acclaimed. Able to quote only one poem of hers, I select what she wrote about Catherine when she was killed:

> *That night, after the day you died,*
> *I heard your voice, cheerfully and close.*
> *I woke, suddenly sobbing as loudly as a child.*
> *Before I slept, I'd driven to the sea.*
> *The moon swirled, through almost colourless*
> *vortices: the mist, off downland fields.*
> *Later, at Christmas-time, my dream*

visited you; you stood, hearing, not speaking,
behind water architecture.
From the lighted front I strained for you
into trellises of mist where in quietness you stood.

Rachel has published eleven novels, revealing an astonishing fertility of imagination. More recently she has made a great mark as a journalist, not to my surprise. On one occasion I took her to visit a prison for the first time. She was soon chatting up a senior prison officer who asked her to come back and see over the prison. Now she is deeply involved in everything penal, and a key member of the New Bridge, actively concerned with *Inside Time*, the paper produced by prisoners. It is an unexpected happiness for me that she should be picking up the torch of penal reform.

Paddy, a classical scholar of Magdalen College, Oxford, and a successful barrister, has during the last three years produced a series of penetrating reports on mental patients for HELP charity of which he is deputy director. Michael, a Cambridge Classicist, is today Minister in Paris. His official despatches will, one gathers, be published one day. I am told, and I am ready to believe, that they are of very high quality. Kevin, a history scholar at New College, Oxford, has alone of those in my extended family (apart from my uncle Arthur Villiers – partner in Barings) displayed his creativity in high finance, or as some would say, in making money, at which the rest of us have not been very good.

And what about the in-laws? Harold Pinter's genius as a playwright needs no encomium from me; his ever greater passion for human rights has brought us close together, as for that matter his love of cricket. For the last twenty years he has taken his own cricket team round the country. Thomas's wife Valerie is a writer admired by all except herself. Rachel's husband Kevin, a leading director of plays, films and television, achieved special eminence as chairman of BAFTA, in which capacity he travelled the world, meeting heads of state in Russia and America.

Michael's wife Mimi had achieved professional acclaim in America before her marriage, as an interior decorator. Within the limitations of being an ambassador's wife she has done distinguished work since that time. Kevin's wife Clare, linguist and publisher, is now recognised as a novelist of a rare subtlety.

I may be asked what of the twenty-six grandchildren and four great-grandchildren? Antonia's two elder daughters, Rebecca and Flora, have written notable biographies. This is getting out of hand. Yet I can't help mentioning that my elder brother Edward wrote a number of plays as well as performing great services to the Gate Theatre, Dublin.

My three surviving sisters, Pansy, Mary and Violet, have all published books; very different but all possessed of a certain distinction. My fourth sister, Julia, who alone of my sisters went to Oxford, was tragically cut off in her early prime. Her son Ferdy is editor of the *Times Literary Supplement*. I might mention again that Violet's husband is Anthony Powell, but enough really is enough.

While on the subject of family – a subject close to my heart – I should like to make known my views about the Prime Minister's rallying cry to the nation, which contains two distinguishable concepts; back to basics and traditional family values. The first could mean anything or nothing, but the second should appeal to all Christians and enlightened Humanists, irrespective of political affiliations. Unfortunately the Prime Minister has thoroughly confused the issue by announcing that personal morality is not involved. To discuss traditional family values without bringing in personal morality is obviously impossible. His new interpretations which hopefully he will in due course reverse makes nonsense of his admirable initiative.

The confusion has been added to by the Conservative Party Chairman, whose message was summed up by the *Sun* under the heading 'Carry on Bonking Fowler tells Tories'. The *Sun* has very properly denounced Sir Norman. I read the *Sun* regularly, and for once I agree with that staunchly Tory newspaper.

I was honoured to be invited to take part in a controversial debate at the Oxford Union on traditional family values.

Given my credentials as a family man, I was rather surprised to be asked to speak against the motion. The President very kindly allowed me to speak in favour of it. We won the debate.

Why should the distinguished lady have thought that I would be opposed to traditional family values? Partly, perhaps, because they have been propounded by a Tory prime minister. More deeply, perhaps, because she assumed that a long-time member of the Labour Party would be against traditions of all kinds. But that would be far too crude. In the course of my eighty-eight years I have naturally seen major developments in Britain. The great improvement in the general standard of life, particularly the redistribution of wealth in favour of the poor (though this trend has been reversed since 1979), is entirely welcome. So is the creation of the Welfare State. We are today a more compassionate society than when I was growing up. I should add that I am an unreconstructed feminist with a deep conviction that all men and women should be treated as equals.

On the other hand, the prison population has increased fivefold since I began visiting in the thirties, and the remorseless growth of crime must be deplored by all of us. At the end of the thirties there were 7,600 divorces a year in Britain; in 1991 there were 153,200. No pseudostatistician will convince me that there is no correlation between these two facts. And to find the true reason for the tremendous increase in the numbers of divorces we must look further than the liberalisation of the divorce laws. The true explanation lies in the serious deterioration in sexual morals. No one will seriously deny that sex before and outside marriage is far commoner that it was fifty years ago, or indeed much more recently than that. The chain of misdemeanour and misfortune is clear enough. Fornication before marriage much increases the risk of adultery afterwards. The broken home and crime follow, not inevitably but in far too many cases.

What do we mean by traditional family values? Fidelity and love are the all-important elements. I am not saying that they always go together, but without fidelity the chances of love sustained over a lifetime are much diminished. The prospects of

189

love and security for the children are correspondingly worsened. I ask the Prime Minister, a decent man as everyone is well aware, to think again and realise that personal morals are at the heart of traditional family values.

22
THE LABOUR PARTY
THEN AND NOW

When I joined the Labour Party in 1936 I told the world that I believed that all men and women were of equal and infinite significance. All my contemporary Socialist friends would have accepted that statement. Some would not have gone along with my addition of the words 'in the sight of God'. But there was also a deep feeling that we were participating, though not ourselves working-class, in a working-class movement. That, no doubt, lay behind Dick Crossman's working-class appeal on behalf of Elizabeth at Cheltenham in 1935. G.D.H. Cole, the most influential Socialist don before the war in Oxford, wrote a massive history of *The Working Class Movement*, pointing to the three distinguishable but united strands; the Labour Party, the trades union movement and the co-operative movement.

Today the Labour Party appeal is seldom couched in purely working-class terms, if only because the proportion of manual workers has so much declined in the last half century. Miners, for example, are now a vanishing breed. Before 1914 more than a million men in this country worked as miners. As far as the Party leadership is concerned, the days of Ernest Bevin and Herbert Morrison have long passed. In the present shadow cabinet I suppose only John Prescott would be labelled a working man if encountered in a railway carriage.

I have often said that the House of Lords has the best

debating and the worst voting system. I have said above that the Labour Party has the best of all political causes and the worst of all political constitutions. The block vote would be ludicrous if it were not a painful reality. No one in their senses could devise such a monstrosity today.

At the time of writing, before his tragic death, John Smith was trying heroically to modify it and, if possible, bring it to an end. It is too much to expect that the trades unions will give up their dominating position without resistance. They can reasonably claim that without them the Labour Party would never have existed. I can only hope and pray that good sense will prevail sooner than later, and the sooner the better.

Others of us discovered, or thought we had discovered, nationalisation or, as it came to be known later, public ownership. We persuaded ourselves that it was more efficient, and appealed to higher human instincts. Before his death, John Smith – to me a most satisfying leader – was playing down the emphasis on the ownership issue. Personally I have always felt, as John Smith seemed to feel, that public ownership is a means to an end, not an end in itself. One way or another it has never stirred me to the depths. I can remember when we were nationalising steel and I, as a junior minister, was helping the Lord Chancellor, Lord Jowett, in the Lords, I went over to the official box and noticed that the civil servant seemed to have two sets of papers in front of him. I could not help asking what the second lot of papers were for. He replied unashamedly, 'They are for denationalising steel when the other lot come in.'

I certainly did not and do not share that degree of cynical detachment. But again, nationalisation one way or the other does not affect my fundamental reasons for being Labour, which are based on social moralities.

I argued in the Lords in 1993 for the adoption by the Labour Party of the principle of Proportional Representation. I admitted, however, that a fine calculation was involved rather than any question of principle. At times I have been out of sympathy with the majority of my Labour colleagues in the Lords and, I suppose, with a majority of Labour MPs.

Abortion would provide an example. Over such matters the Labour Party has scrupulously allowed a free vote according to conscience. In 1967, as already described, I left my seat as Leader of the House and spoke against the Abortion Bill. But that Bill, like most others of its kind, was officially a private member's product. As I write, 'opportunities for all' are being given top priority as a keynote of Labour policy in the coming years. Hugh Gaitskell, when Leader of the House in the late 1950s, said that Socialism was about equality. John Smith would certainly not deny the truth in Gaitskell's words, but he is seeking to provide an inspiration to the nation as a whole.

In the thirty-four years from the end of the war to the coming of Thatcherism in 1979, there was steady movement under both Conservative and Labour governments to distribute income more equally. From 1979, that movement has been reversed. Personally I should never be satisfied with any Labour Party policy that did not make the distribution more and more equal. The time may come when that movement may have to be halted – not, I predict, in the lifetime of the youngest of us.

I can honestly say that I have been happy at all times in my life in the Labour Party, even when some of its policies have differed from those I would have preferred. Twenty years of Clem Attlee's leadership was a bonus I hardly valued enough at the time. Tucked away in the Lords and leaving London at the weekend, I was never one of the inner Gaitskellite political circles, though he referred to me on occasion as 'his oldest friend'. His humane agnosticism admittedly bothered me. When he became Leader of the Party I wrote to ask whether he minded my praying for him. He replied, 'Of course I don't mind, we are closer than you think.' I have never been sure what he meant or how he would have moved on that plane if he had been spared.

If Hugh had lived it was quite likely he would have secured an extension of the Bill enabling a hereditary peer to give up his title. Under such a plan, I would have been able to abandon my peerage of First Creation and stand for the Commons. But I am not sorry that that chance was denied me. I would not have been able to pursue the causes which, in my own eyes, have given a genuine meaning to my public life.

I have kept repeating that I am a Christian Socialist. It is worth saying one word about Christianity in the Labour Party. It has often been said that the Party owed more to Methodism than Marxism, but that is an exiguous claim. I feel intense rapport with Donald Soper, ninety-one this year, and still speaking away without a microphone at Speakers' Corner and Tower Hill. Donald always insists that Christianity leads to Socialism and Socialism to pacifism. I can't go along with the last part of that affirmation, but the first part accords with my own convictions.

Nevertheless it is an historic fact that much of the ideology of the Labour Party was formulated by the Fabians, who cannot be credited with Christian beliefs in spite of Beatrice Webb's Christian strivings. The truth is that non-denominational Christianity has been a large part of the inspiration of the Labour Party, but there have been other vital elements. It was a source of deep personal satisfaction to me that our last leader, John Smith, was a dedicated Christian Socialist.

The attitude of the Labour Party to the outside world deserves attention. I did not join the Party because of their international policy. On the whole, over the years, that attitude has strengthened my Labour convictions, but that has not been invariably true. In the 1980s, Labour espoused a form of semi-pacifism, although they would not have accepted that title. Heresy has been abandoned, and first under Neil Kinnock and then under John Smith they have, in international affairs, returned to the tradition of Clem Attlee and Ernest Bevin.

It should be recalled that for two periods, from 1932 to 1939 and from 1952 to 1954, I taught among other subjects, international history, 1871–1914, and international relations from 1918 onwards. Quite apart from my political activities, these studies, not surprisingly, affected me profoundly. I owed many but by no means all of my ideas to Woodrow Wilson, to the international anarchy of Lowes Dickinson and to de Valera, whom I so much admired. I emerged with three convictions: 1. That collective security was the only ultimate clue to world peace; 2. That law and order, while indispensable, were not the total answer in international affairs, but must at all costs be supplemented by international justice; 3. That the right to self-determination, with all its ambiguities, was an ideal for which individual human beings would worthily lay down their lives, although on occasion its assertion would bring about more harm than good.

In 1935, though not yet a member of the Labour Party, I attended the historic party conference. The leader at that time was George Lansbury, a noted pacifist, and the Party as a whole had not yet made up its mind as to whether Collective Security, the underlying principle of the League of Nations, could be achieved on pacifist lines. I shall never forget the ringing declaration of George Lansbury: 'As Jesus Christ said in the Garden, "Those who live by the sword, shall perish by the sword." There I have made my stand, and there, if necessary, I shall die.'

The whole assembly rose and cheered for many minutes. But then Ernest Bevin, carrying the block vote in his pocket, stumped to the rostrum and countered roughly, 'I am not going to have George Lansbury hawking his conscience all round Europe.' The block vote prevailed. Although I dislike the whole concept of the block vote, I am bound to say that I thought it worked well on this occasion. Lansbury resigned the leadership, to be succeeded by Clem Attlee, then still known as Major Attlee, who, in Churchill's generous words, had 'been through the heaviest fighting in the war'.

From that day onwards for many years, Labour stood for effective defence in the interests of world security. Emotionally, however, a long-standing dislike of militarism persisted. At the conference just mentioned, Stafford Cripps, the idol of the Left, was yet another speaker who brought the house down when he declared, 'I am never going to ask the workers of this country to put themselves back under the military machine.' There was less than no sympathy for me when I joined the Territorials in the spring of 1939. The Labour Party was still opposing conscription at that time.

I was in the gallery on one occasion when Bevin declared that he would never allow Poland to be thrown to the wolves (though in fact he could not prevent this happening). He was cheered by the Conservatives, but heard in silence on his own side of the House.

Hugh Gaitskell passionately believed in the Atlantic Alliance and in close friendship with the United States. When Harold Wilson succeeded him, some of us feared that position would be weakened. This did not happen; he reappointed Patrick Gordon Walker as foreign affairs spokesman and, in all his years of leadership, proved himself as firm an ally of the United States as Gaitskell, although he may have used different language.

Under the leadership of Michael Foot and Neil Kinnock in his earlier days, there was a strong movement towards unilateral nuclear disarmament. In the 1980s, although I remained President of the Battle and Bexhill Labour Party, I would have found it difficult to stand as a candidate. Those days are now, I hope, forgotten, and the tradition of Attlee and Bevin resumed. The collapse of the Soviet Union has simplified the main issue – while creating a hundred lesser headaches.

In the thirties, and for a long time after the war, the issue of Europe did not disturb the Labour Party. As recounted above, the suggestion Dr Adenauer made through me to Attlee and Bevin in 1950, that they should join the original Iron and Steel Pact, was treated with disdain.

As the fifties receded, however, the movement towards Europe proceeded on various levels in Britain. The Treasury, the Board of Trade and later, it would seem, the Foreign Office, moved steadily in that direction. Dedicated Europeans emerged among Labour leaders, such as George Brown and Roy Jenkins. I can well remember a vehement, highly intellectual debate at a fringe meeting of the Labour conference in 1962; Roy Jenkins for Europe, Douglas Jay against. Thirty years later the same two champions are jousting away with a similar antagonism in the Lords.

On the day following that debate, Hugh Gaitskell made a tremendous speech, which was definitely regarded as anti- rather than pro-Europe, although he would have claimed that it was balanced. When he sat down, I asked Michael Stewart, who was sitting beside me, 'What did you think of that?' He replied in his usual, careful fashion, 'I tend to agree with him, but I think that he rather over-stated his case.'

When the Labour government was formed in 1964 (Hugh, alas, having died at the beginning of 1963), it did not seem at first that Labour would move in the direction of Europe. I was speaking fairly often at that time as Leader of the House on foreign affairs. I was conscious that the Foreign Office was anxious for me to be more and more pro-European in my utterances. George Brown and the Foreign Office gradually obtained a majority in the cabinet on an approach to Europe, Douglas Jay resisting to the end and losing his cabinet seat in consequence. I will not travel over the subsequent attitude of the Party to Europe, which was for many years equivocal at best.

John Smith and Ivor Richard, our very capable leaders in Parliament in these latter days, were always strongly pro-European. I have been told by those who were present at the TUC conference that the address given by Jacques Delors was a turning point.

23
ELIZABETH

If it is difficult for me to offer an objective view of the House of Lords, it is impossible for me to offer one of Elizabeth. But I will dream the impossible dream and imagine a national contest for the most remarkable woman of my time. My shortlist would begin with Edna O'Brien, nominated by Elizabeth for her beauty and imagination, but she is Irish so she can't win. That leaves me with Margaret Thatcher and Elizabeth. Under the heading of achievement it is impossible not to award the palm to Lady Thatcher, three times Prime Minister. Elizabeth was told both by Ernest Bevin and Hugh Dalton that if she had persevered with her political career she would have been elected to the National Executive of the Labour Party. Who knows what might have happened after that? She gave it all up for the sake of the family. Still, there is no getting away from Margaret Thatcher's place in the political history of Britain.

Margaret Thatcher's memoirs have sold enormously but she would be the last to compare them to Elizabeth's contribution to literature. When it comes to children, grandchildren and great-grandchildren, Elizabeth ranks supreme. Elizabeth, like Antonia, is notably generous to fellow writers. The Catherine Pakenham Memorial Prize for young women journalists, initiated originally by Jonathan Aitken, has been a huge success. The support of the *Evening Standard*, now of the *Sunday Telegraph* under the enthusiastic leadership of Charles Moore, has been invaluable. Valerie Grove has been a tower of strength. She and others concerned, including the prize-winners, have been aware at all times of Elizabeth's infectious kindness.

I can recommend all Elizabeth's books, and not only because they have been dedicated to me. Her lives of Victoria, Wellington, Byron, the Queen Mother and the Queen are known to all. Not so well known as it should be is *Poet's Corner* (1992), an anthology of prose and poetry by those commemorated at Westminster Abbey. Elizabeth's long introduction is a reminder that English literature was her first love, a subject in which she won an open scholarship to Lady Margaret Hall, Oxford. One passage must suffice to give the flavour: 'My choices of Wordsworth were firmly fixed by visits to the "Wordsworth Country": reading aloud "Tintern Abbey" in situ, and other poems in places where he had lived. Shelley in a sense presented me with the least of my problems. I could never forget the effect of first reading his "Prometheus Unbound". This poem, together with Shakespeare's *Hamlet*, gave me the same kind of thrill as Keats felt on first looking into Chapman's Homer. So I had to have a passage from it . . .'

I have not introduced a family criterion into my Judgment of Paris. Elizabeth has seven surviving children and numerous grand- and great-grandchildren, to all of whom she sends presents every Christmas and on every birthday. She remembers our beloved Catherine at all times. She is not likely to come second in a family competition.

The annual Garter ceremony lunch at Windsor Castle, the parade down to the chapel and the service there have meant as much to Elizabeth as to me. Elizabeth has emerged beyond question as the leading Royal biographer. She has written seven books altogether on Royal subjects; *Victoria R.I.* won the 1964 James Tait Black Memorial Prize. Her most recent book, *Royal Throne: The Future of the Monarchy,* is a triumph. I would never have forecast such an apotheosis when she was a young woman; nor, I am sure, would she.

To quote from *Royal Throne*: 'Brought up in a non-conformist family on both sides, I imagined that Church and State represented exclusion and opposition for the likes of us. One idea which never entered my head was that the country's contentious, divided people and interests could be held together by the Crown.' Then came the opportunity, originally embraced in a spirit of historical detachment, to work in the Royal Archives at Windsor for her book on Victoria. *Royal Throne* continues: 'During the four busy exciting years I spent researching among Queen Victoria's family papers I gained a consuming interest in Victorian families in general and the Royal family in particular, developing a firm belief in the monarchy's constitutional role.' She, therefore, is that fairly rare phenomenon, a dedicated monarchist and a dedicated radical. Harold Wilson, who seems to have been a special favourite with the Queen, might be another such.

As a profound admirer of President de Valera in Ireland, I would not claim to be a sentimental monarchist. But I am convinced beyond all argument that it is vital for Britain that the monarchy should continue to prosper. Elizabeth and I share a deep admiration for the Queen and, may I add, for Prince Charles. Of all the valuable sections of *Royal Throne* I find the description of Prince Charles and his preparation for his future role as king perhaps the most valuable of all.

I feel a kind of duty to quote Mary Craig's assessment of me as a Garter Knight: 'In a very real way Frank's role as Knight of the Garter symbolised his basic ambivalence. He has never decided to which world he belongs. While he has continued to take a childish delight in the aura and trappings of privilege – yet he sits loose to it and cannot take it seriously. Pride in the honour that has been bestowed on him, and he has a deep need for the assurance that it affords, battles with an awareness that all worldly honours are ultimately ludicrous.'

It is, no doubt, healthy to see ourselves as others see us especially when the 'other' is as perceptive a friend as Mary, though 'ludicrous' is perhaps too strong a word to describe any feelings of mine. I will only add that John Hunt when invited to become a Knight of the Garter assumed that the letter was intended for Lord Hunt and proposed to send it on to him. I had no such inhibitions. I grabbed this supreme honour before it could run away from me and have never ceased to be intensely proud to have been selected by the Queen for this purpose.

I will not dwell on the joyous side of sixty-two years of happy marriage. I will confine describing Elizabeth's support at sombre moments. When, under her influence, I joined the Labour Party in 1936, I had already been described as a 'dud' Conservative. I would have drifted into political oblivion. As I have explained, I was deeply humiliated by my wartime collapse in the army. In times to come, confronted with so many people failed or fallen into disgrace, I could see it as a blessing in disguise; throughout the war, to use Churchill's expression after defeat in the 1945 election, 'the blessing was well disguised'.

In 1947 I was much distressed by my failure to make my resignation effective over British policy towards Germany; and in 1968 by the isolation into which I fell after resigning from the Wilson cabinet. In 1971–2 I was overwhelmed with ridicule in intellectual circles through my anti-pornography crusade and later, for a number of years, with something like hatred in the tabloid press through my defence of Myra Hindley. At all these times, Elizabeth's strength of character was indispensable to my survival. Sir Thomas More called his wife, Dame Alice (not in all respects an attractive figure), a lioness. Elizabeth has been for me not only a lioness but a loving lioness throughout.

24
FAINT BUT
PURSUING

All my life I have been some kind of Christian, since my first prayer taught by my mother. For more than half a century I have been a practising Catholic, and I am more grateful than I can say to my family and my Church. I would not, however, describe myself as deeply religious. I would apply such a phrase to Malcolm and Kitty Muggeridge, as they were at the end of their lives. By that time they could fairly have been described as mystics.

Elizabeth and I were delighted but much surprised when Malcolm told us one evening at his home near Robertsbridge that he and Kitty were to be received into the Catholic Church. They wanted us to be their sponsors, and we of course accepted with alacrity. It seemed too good to be true. When we returned to Bernhurst in 1950 we saw Malcolm and Kitty almost every weekend until Malcolm's death. They became our dear and sparkling friends, irrespective of religion.

By 1969 Malcolm, with his book *Jesus Rediscovered*, had emerged as a Christian champion of rare eloquence. By the eighties, with his writings and above all his television programmes, he had become the most effective Christian apologist of his time. Elizabeth and I were aware of his profound admiration of Mother Theresa. I gather now that he gave her cause the £50,000 which he earned by his book about her. And Malcolm was never remotely a rich man. But by the

1980s it seemed to us unlikely that he would ever accept the discipline of the Catholic or any other Church. Thus the news of his impending reception filled us with unrestrained joy.

The Reverend John Stott, taking the chair for Malcolm's lectures on Christ and the Media, said of him: 'The publication of *Jesus Rediscovered* in 1969 told the world of his personal commitment to Jesus Christ, while in *Jesus, the Man who Lives* (1975) his Christian faith is seen to burn more brightly still.'

An earlier perspective was provided by Sir Brian Young, director-general of the Independent Broadcasting Authority. (Malcolm had been very severe in his lecture on television in spite of his own proficiency in the art.) Young recorded: 'Twenty years ago, as editor of *Punch*, he published something so shocking to that magazine's old public, that one of them, my father, cancelled his subscriptions and wrote to Malcolm Muggeridge to protest that, in passion to satisfy a rootless and immoral public, he was sweeping away all decent standards.'

The reactions of his friends and critics to his so-called 'late conversion' to Christianity have been better described by Malcolm than by anyone else. 'There is a very funny book to be written about becoming a Christian in the last decades of the twentieth century . . . In senility, the poor fellow, they say, shaking their heads sadly; used to be quite amusing until this unaccountable aberration seized him, since when, it must be admitted, he has been an unconscionable bore.' He went on to say, 'Others not so amicably inclined look for some more sinister explanation, expatiating upon how old lechers when they become impotent are notoriously liable to denounce lechery, seeking to deprive others of pleasures no longer within their reach.'

Malcolm has said that he never underwent 'any dramatic change'. But certainly there was, in a short space of time, a dramatic change in his conduct, although he was in a sense the same delightful companion before and after his 'conversion'. Before it he was, to put it mildly, very liberal in his approach to women in spite of a beautiful lifelong marriage to Kitty. He drank heavily, he smoked like a chimney and, incidentally, ate meat like the rest of us. When he became an articulate Christian he cut out wine, women and tobacco and became a rigid vegetarian. No ascetic ever put his theories into practice more completely.

At the end of his book, *Christ and the Media*, embodying his lectures on that subject, he summarised what he called his 'operational orders':

1 Seek endlessly for God and for his hand in all creatures.

2 Live abstemiously.

3 Live and consider all men and women as brothers and sisters, caring for them exactly as we should for Jesus himself.

4 Read the Bible and related literature, especially mystical, like the metaphysical poets and *The Cloud of Unknowing*.

5 Know Jesus Christ and follow his way like Bunyan's Pilgrim, withersoever it may lead.

No one ever stated the Christian teaching more succinctly nor, at the end of his life, with Kitty, a truly splendid woman, always at his side, lived up to his message more faithfully.

It would be extraordinary if those who set themselves a Christian standard of conduct did not behave better by Christian standards than those who make no such commitment. A brilliant circle such as the Bloomsbury set with doctrines such as that of 'free love', cannot satisfy Christian commentators. But they may well have preferred their own form of morals to that of Christians. There are exceptions to all rules, like Attlee who, accepting 'the Christian ethic', couldn't 'stand the mumbo jumbo' but whose main influence in adult life was his brother Tom, a Christian pacifist.

How far my own professed Christianity and compliance with the Christian rules have affected my personal conduct I must leave others to judge. But there can be no doubt about the dominant effect of my Christianity on my public attitudes – to Germany, pornography, prisoners and mental offenders. I will say again, I am a Socialist because I am a Christian.

When I last made that statement in the Lords, I was quick to acknowledge that there were better Christians than myself in the House. I pointed to Baroness Cox, on the opposite side. I recalled that the inclusion of the word Christianity in the Education Act of 1989 was entirely due to her initiative. Caroline Cox, former nurse and polytechnic lecturer, dashes off at a moment's notice to take medical supplies to some of the most dangerous, war-stricken areas in Africa and Asia. Among Labour colleagues I created no surprise by pointing to the Reverend Donald Soper who has preached Christianity in the open air for sixty years.

In 1989 I produced a small book called *Forgiveness of Man by Man*. The views I expressed remain mine today. Forgiveness, along with humility, I would describe as the most distinctive Christian virtue, though Christians claim that the concept of love or charity is wider and deeper in Christianity than any-where else. As with humility, I had found it almost impossible to find a systematic book on the subject. In 1927 Professor Mackintosh produced his impressive *Christian Experience of Forgiveness*, but it is concerned almost entirely with forgive-ness of man by God. Forgiveness of man by man hardly figured.

This second aspect of forgiveness of man by God was not neglected.

I myself have never been placed in the position of having to try to forgive someone who had done me a serious wrong. My greatly loved daughter, Catherine, was killed through the neg-ligence of the young man driving the car in which she was travelling. He was killed himself, but if he had survived, I hon-estly do not think that I would have cherished ill-will towards him. On the other hand, if Catherine had been murdered, who knows? I can only hope that I would have sublimated my natural feelings, as have many others, for example in Northern Ireland.

In public affairs the issue of forgiveness has come my way many times. I finished my book on the Anglo-Irish Treaty with the words: 'Whatever England's policy, it remains for Ireland to do herself justice as a nation, for that she has not yet done.

It remains for England to make atonement. For that she has not yet made.' Over the last eight hundred years, Ireland has had much to forgive. Since I wrote, however, many individual wrongs have been committed by individuals on all sides in Northern Ireland. The search today for a general balance of wrongdoing is not a profitable undertaking.

In my book I quoted individuals on all sides of the argument who illustrate the forgiving spirit. I was introduced to a number of them by my friend Anne Tanny, who took me well below the surface. Among them, Gordon Wilson, the Methodist draper of Enniskillin, has achieved world fame much against his will. His beloved daughter was murdered in a bomb outrage. He himself had a narrow escape from death. Afterwards he issued his noble proclamation: 'My wife and I do not hold any ill-will against those responsible for this. We see it as God's plan, even though we might not understand it. I shall pray for those people tonight and every night. God forgive them, for they know not what they do.' He added, 'All I know is that we have lost a gorgeous girl.'

When I was sent to Germany in 1947, I was inspired by men like Dr Bell, Bishop of Chichester, Richard Stokes, MP, Victor Gollancz and Michael de la Bedoyère, editor of the *Catholic Herald.* I did my best to preach an unequivocal doctrine of forgiveness. But I did not represent the official policy of the time. For almost the only time in my life I felt guided from above; yet I was not strong enough to live up to my guidance.

Three problems concerned me especially in my book, as they must any serious student of forgiveness. First, is it possible to forgive anyone who has not harmed us directly, or indirectly? The Vicar of Ealing had immediately forgiven those who had beaten him up, but did not think it right for him to try to forgive those who had raped a young woman in his house. I submitted and still submit that, with deep respect to the vicar, such a limitation of forgiveness would rule out all forgiveness by communities such as the Jews who have in many cases, though not of course in all, not suffered themselves. It still seems inconceivable to me that a Christian will rule out the idea of community forgiveness.

The second problem is whether it is a duty to forgive some-

206

one before he or she has repented. But when Jesus Christ told Peter he should forgive a neighbour up to seventy times seven, that is to say indefinitely, he seemed to rule out the notion of waiting until the neighbour had repented. When he said on the Cross, 'Father, forgive them for they know not what they do', it is an unqualified request, not one dependent on the attitude of those who needed to be forgiven. A further consideration weighs with me heavily. In half a century of prison visiting I have been asked repeatedly whether such and such a prisoner feels remorse, or has repented. It is a bold man who reconsiders himself capable of judging the degree of repentance or remorse of his fellow human.

Thirdly, and this is the most difficult of the questions, there is a whole problem of combining forgiveness with punishment. My answer is simple: punishment is part of Christian justice, but sentences and the administration of justice in prison must at all times be guided by love. An impossible aspiration, if you like. But the only standard by which to judge a penal system.

A year later, I wrote another small book, entitled *Suffering and Hope*. As mentioned earlier, I had intended to call it *Suffering* but my most percipient editor, Teresa de Bertodano, rightly persuaded me that a message of hope was involved. Better written than any contribution of mine was Elizabeth's *Prelude*, which can only be briefly quoted from here. About the loss of Catherine, aged twenty-three, which she has written of in her own memoirs, she said starkly, 'Belief in God saved me from pouring out the most negative of all griefs and grievances: Why me?' Of the physical pain involved in an operation for the removal of a benign tumour she wrote, 'I was given the gift of experiencing utter dependence on others . . . I was learning about my total dependence on God in all humility.'

The little book is crammed with brief, unforgettable contributions from many quarters. Three who wrote about hospices for the dying have already been quoted. I will add quotations from three other sufferers. 'Suffering,' wrote Mary Craig, 'is the key to discovery of what we are and what we have in us to become. If only we can summon the strength.' 'While', writes Sister Frances Makower, 'on the more superficial level I fight both pain and dependence, deep down I find myself grateful for my situation which draws me ever closer to the pierced heart of Christ . . .' Margaret Spufford tells us that if we think of the glorified Lord as the disciples saw him before the Ascension, 'We may start thinking of the beauty of God achieved not in spite of pain by somehow through it.' It was an uncovenanted privilege for me to be allowed to question such splendid witnesses from first-hand experience of the Christian view of suffering.

I began that book by asking a few questions. How do we explain suffering? How do we bear our own suffering? How do we relieve the suffering of others? I do not claim to have answered any of those everlasting questions conclusively. No one but a madman would make such a claim. I have placed much reliance on mystery as a residual element. Believing Christians will not be disturbed. They will rely on the confident hope that all will be made plain in the world to come. They will not feel envious of the wise men of other religions, or the atheists or agnostics quoted here. I hope, however, that I have provided significant examples of the extraordinary inspiration provided in the face of suffering by Christian belief. By setting forth the capacity of these human beings to unite their sufferings with those of Christ, and their awareness of the presence of the Holy Spirit, I have dwelt on the prodigious efforts made under Christian inspiration towards the relief of suffering in any shape.

And what of Catholic policy today? In one respect, I feel sure that the official line will be altered. I refer to the ordination of women. As an ardent feminist, I cannot understand how it would be possible in the long run to exclude half the human race from the priesthood. If I am reminded that Jesus Christ did not appoint women apostles, I draw attention to the passage in Matthew, where we are told that five thousand men were fed, *excluding women and children.* At that time it would have been inconceivable that women would have been placed in official positions in the Church. We are not likely to forget that it was the women, rather than the men, who remained faithful to Christ on the Cross.

I write these words painfully aware that the present Pope has expressed very different views. My regret is all the greater because my reverence for him, quite apart from his official position, stops only just short of idolatry. In 1981 I had the wonderful privilege of interviewing him for a book I was commissioned to write about him, which (I cannot help mentioning) eventually won the *Universe* Prize for the best religious book of the year. I heard him speak when he visited these islands in Dublin and Knock and Westminster Cathedral.

I took the prudent step when visiting him in Rome of equipping myself with a message from our parish priest. I began by announcing, after kneeling to kiss his ring, 'I bring a message of profound respect and admiration from Father Maxwell, parish priest of Hurst Green.' He repeated with evident satisfaction, more than once, 'Father Maxwell, parish priest of Hurst Green.' It did not need the tremendous addresses that I heard him deliver later to assure me that here was a man of universal love.

Towards the end of 1993 the Pope issued the encyclical *Veritatis Splendor*, which was heralded by much misleading comment in the British press. It was widely suggested that he was laying his main emphasis on artificial birth control, for example, which in fact the encyclical only mentions in passing. Fortunately for Catholics in Britain, the bishops issued a clarifying statement which enabled the man in the pew to feel that nothing new was expected. In that case it may reasonably be asked why was it thought necessary to issue the encyclical at all. The short answer would seem to be that the Pope was determined to insist that moral values were unchanging, as against the views of some Catholic theologians which seemed to favour a certain relativity in accordance with changing cultures.

For myself I find no difficulty in believing that what was right and wrong yesterday is right and wrong today. I find much more difficulty in the concept of absolute norms which admit of no exceptions. What of the mother who steals to feed her starving children? I cherish the belief that in such a situation the present Pope would be as compassionate as his master.

As I conclude I ask myself to whom I would award Victoria Crosses among those I have known, from the point of view of Christianity. I leave out Elizabeth and the rest of my family; I

209

leave out those who pursue a religious vocation; I leave out the statesmen I most admire, and also Leonard Cheshire, whom I described shortly before his death as the greatest living Englishman. I confine myself to those who have done noble work in the face of affliction or disaster.

In the House of Lords, I think of members confined for life to wheelchairs who have for many years spread a spirit of gaiety and courage. Outside the House, I think of one who was sadly eliminated from high politics and has done splendid work ever since among the poorest. I think of one who was imprisoned in a remote country and is now the life and soul of a hospice. I think of one who had a total mental breakdown when young and has done more than any other individual for mental sufferers. I think also of those who responded bravely to poignant family situations which would have crushed most of us.

I do not compete with such as these. I would take as my model Nicodemus, who crept out of the shadows to assist Joseph of Arimathea to bury Jesus Christ. Theirs has been finely described as the hour of the timid. I would not claim to have had my hour, but, lovingly supported, I have had my moments. I cannot refrain from pointing also to the example of Father Damien who washed the feet of the lepers as his master once washed those of the disciples. His values are those above all others which I offer to the present generation and to the generation to come.

'He who would be great should be as a minister. He who would be first should be as he who serves.'

POSTSCRIPT

June 1994

At the very moment that this book was going to press came the tragic news of John Smith's death. What was written about him has needed some last-minute revision, but nothing will ever change my mind that he would have made a great prime minister. He will be awaiting with confidence now the triumph of the Party that he loved so deeply.

Still later, at an advanced stage in the book's production, I heard with great sorrow that Frank Beck had died suddenly. After his death I received a letter, written shortly before, which I shall always treasure, and the poem from which I can only quote four lines below. His appeal has obviously had to be dropped and I shall continue to hope that the efforts to clear his name will be successful.

> *Then to die, by someone's evil streak.*
> *A flickering light, always cold,*
> *A light no more, now by God's grace,*
> *Free for sure.*

INDEX

writing 2: *Born to Believe* 4, 97; *Forgiveness of Man by Man* 63, 157, 205; *Humility* 133; *Eleven at Number Ten* 175, 180; history of House of Lords 175; *Causes of Crime* 4; *The Idea of Punishment* 159; *Peacemakers* 175; on Pope John Paul II 1; *Prisoner or Patient* 140, 159, 163, 168; *Peace by Ordeal* 3, 60, 69, 75; *Punishment and the Punished* 159; lives of US Presidents 175–80; *Young Offenders* 175; *Peacemakers* 175; *Suffering and Hope* 133, 207
Longford, Countess of (Elizabeth Pakenham) 2, 17, 21, 25, 29, 44, 46, 47, 50, 53–8, 60, 62, 72, 75–6, 78–81, 82, 85, 86–7, 91, 110, 112, 114, 119, 126, 130, 141, 148, 149, 157, 160, 184, 190, 197–200, 201, 209: marries Francis Pakenham 57, 66; politics and 56, 70, 78–9, 81, 100; religion and 79, 81–2; as writer 115, 146, 176, 184, 186, 198–9, 207

McDonald, Gregory 32
MacDonald, Ramsay 177
McGraw Eric 121–2
MacKenzie, Kelvin 157, 158
McNaughton, H.V. 35
MacNeice, Louis 87
Mackilligin, Jenny 151
Mackintosh, Professor 205
Macmillan, Harold l9, 39, 46, 176, 179, 180–81, 185
Maine, Sir Henry 52
Major, John l9, 100, 116, 140, 151, 153, 163, 175, 177, 180, 181, 184–5, 188, 189
Makins, Roger (Lord Sheffield) 24
Makower, Sister Frances 207
Mallalieu, Ann 140, 162
Manningham-Buller, Reginald (Lord Dilhorne) 35
Margesson, David 94
Marshall, General 106
Martelli, George 25
Masham, Lady Susan 144
Masterman, J.C. 80
Masterson, John 162
Matthew, Trust 2, 169
Maudling, Reginald 161
Maxwell, Father 209
Mayhew, Christopher 78, 83, 84–5, 111
Mencap 1–2, 143
Miller, Keith 32
Milton, Frank 120
MIND 151
Molotov, Mr 106
Montgomery, Viscount 102–3, 105
Moore, Bobby 30
Moore, Charles 198
Morris, Alfred 142, 143
Morrison, Herbert 110–11, 124, 191
Mortimer, John 153
Mortimer, Raymond 2
Mosley, Lady Diana 72–3, 147
Mosley, Sir Oswsld 45–6, 66, 71–2, 147
Mottram, Ruth 131
Mountbatten, Lord Louis 96–7, 110, 148
Moyne, Lord (Bryan) *see* Guinness, Bryan
Moyne, Lord (Jonathan) 73
Muggeridge, Kitty 201, 202, 203
Muggeridge, Malcolm 154, 201–3
Murdoch, Rupert 156–7

Murray, Basil 71
Murray, Lady 84
Murray, Professor Gilbert 71, 84
Mussolini, Benito 68, 72, 109

Nathan, Sir Harry 144
National Society for the Mentally Handicapped *see* Mencap
National Viewers' and Listeners' Association 152–3
Nevinson, H.W. 20
New Bridge 1, 4, 121–2, 159, 162, 187
New Horizon youth centre 1, 30, 48, 64–5, 129, 142–3, 147, 154, 155
Newton, Nigel 146
Nichol, Wendy 141
Nilsen, Dennis 162–4, 168, 170
Nixon, Richard 163–4, 176, 179–80
Noel-Baker, Philip 86
Nuffield Foundation 120

O'Brien, Edna 198
O'Brien, Murrough 80
O'Cathain, Detta 140
O'Connell, Daniel 117
O'Docherty, Shane 63
Oliver, Major Matthew 155–6
Oliver, Vivienne 155–6
O'Neill, Dr Tom 63
Opie, Robert 83, 115
O'Reilly, Tony 39

Paisley, Rev. Ian 63
Pakenham, Antonia (daughter) *see* Pinter, Antonia
Pakenham, Arthur 74
Pakenham, Catherine (daughter) 62, 79 186, 199, 205, 207
Pakenham, Charles Reginald (later Paul Mary) 10–11
Pakenham, Christine 55
Pakenham, Clare 74, 188
Pakenham, General 9, 89
Pakenham, Judith (daughter) 74, 79, 115, 186
Pakenham, Julia (sister) 10, 188
Pakenham, Kevin (son) 73, 79, 117, 187, 188
Pakenham, Kitty 9
Pakenham, Mary (sister) 6, 30–31, 188
Pakenham, Michael (son) 79, 87, 187–8
Pakenham, Mimi 87, 184, 187–8
Pakenham, Pansy (sister) 6, 10, 97, 188
Pakenham, Patrick ('Paddy') (son) 79, 187
Pakenham, Rachel (daughter) 79, 115, 130, 187
Pakenham, Thomas (son) 3, 10, 34, 79, 146, 186, 187
Pakenham, Violet (sister) 10, 55, 188
Pakenham, Valerie 187
Palliser, Michael 87
Pinter, Antonia 7, 34, 72, 79, 85, 94, 115, 146, 175, 178, 186, 188
Pinter, Harold 33, 35–6, 187
Pollitt, Harry 77
Powell, Anthony 10, 15, 55–6, 188
Powell, Enoch 132
Prescott, John 191
Procter, Bill 145–6
Profumo, Jack 47–8
Profumo, Valerie 48